BRAIN CACH

Dr Gareth Moore B.Sc (Hons) M.Phil Ph.D is the internationally best-selling author of a wide range of brain-training and puzzle books for both children and adults, including *Enigma: Crack the Code*, *Ultimate Dot to Dot*, *Brain Games for Clever Kids*, *Lateral Logic* and *Extreme Mazes*. His books have sold over a million copies in the UK alone, and have been published in over thirty different languages. He is also the creator of online brain-training site BrainedUp.com, and runs the daily puzzle site PuzzleMix.com.

BRAIN CACH

TRAIN, REGAIN AND MAINTAIN YOUR MENTAL AGILITY IN
40 DAYS

DR GARETH MOORE

Michael O'Mara Books Limited

First published in Great Britain in 2019 by
Michael O'Mara Books Limited
9 Lion Yard
Tremadoc Road
London SW4 7NQ

A CIP catalogue record for this book is available from the
British Library.

Papers used by Michael O'Mara Books Limited are natural,
recyclable products made from wood grown in sustainable
forests. The manufacturing processes conform to the
environmental regulations of the country of origin.

ISBN: 978-1-78929-019-6 in paperback print format

1 2 3 4 5 6 7 8 9 10

Designed and typeset by Gareth Moore

Printed and bound by CPI Group (UK) Ltd, Croydon, CR0 4YY

www.mombooks.com

CONTENTS

INTRODUCTION

Welcome to *Brain Coach: Train, Regain and Maintain Your Mental Agility in 40 Days*. By reading just a couple of pages a day, and doing the two or so exercises associated with each day, you can transform your brain skills in less than a month and a half.

You *are* your brain. Without it, you can't do a thing. It is a microcosm of the universe, brimming with potential and just waiting for you to take full advantage of it. Given its critical role in every aspect of our being, surely we should be looking after it?

In this day-by-day programme I will take you on a journey through your brain, using small, simple steps that draw on the latest science to help you learn how to make greater use of your innate abilities. A deeper understanding of how your brain works can help you in all aspects of life, from making better decisions through to thinking smarter, faster thoughts.

The book is complemented by the inclusion of a specially designed range of brain games, so you can immediately put into practice many of the techniques that the book describes. And, of course, the 40 days you spend on the book need not be consecutive – they can be spread out and fitted in as you have time. In fact, some of the activities might easily take you more than a single session to complete.

Full solutions to the exercises, where relevant, are given at the back of the book.

CARE FOR YOUR BRAIN

+ It's important to take care of your brain
+ Your brain thrives on new experiences and challenges
+ Unused brain circuitry is discarded

WHAT?

You can look in a mirror and see your body, and you know exactly how you feel as you move, so you have a good idea as to how physically healthy you are. But what about your brain? It's much harder to assess the state of your brain, but looking after it is every bit as important as looking after your body.

Constantly challenge your brain so it continues to learn, building new ways to think. Your brain uses a large amount of the body's energy, and unused parts may be discarded by your brain's natural housekeeping processes.

WHY?

No matter your intelligence, you need to care for your brain at least as much as your body. Without it, you can't do anything.

Suggested time to spend
15 MINUTES

YOUR BRAIN

When you were small, your brain grew rapidly. It gained brain cells and the connections between them at a fearsome rate, as you experienced the world around you. At puberty, your brain cleaned itself up, throwing away a huge number of connections that had been made but not much used.

Your brain reached (or, if you're young enough, *will* reach) its peak performance in your mid-20s. After this age, it's a downhill ride – but you are in control of the speed of that ride. Look after your brain and it could be fairly level terrain, but fail to do so and you'll accelerate towards old age with ever-decreasing mental abilities.

BRAIN CARE

Look after your brain by:

▶ Challenging yourself as often as you can

▶ Seeking variety and new experiences

▶ Eating a varied diet, including all recommended vitamins, minerals, essential fatty acids and essential amino acids

▶ Being physically fit, so your brain has a steady and regular supply of oxygen

▶ Looking after your mental health

These are easy to write and sometimes hard to do, but you only have one brain – and only you have the power to look after it.

DAY 1: EXERCISE 1

Start your programme of brain improvement with this challenging puzzle that you are unlikely to have seen before.

To solve it, draw 1x2 and 1x3 rectangular blocks along the grid lines so that each number is contained in exactly one block.

▶ The number in each block reveals the total count of white spaces the block can slide into. Shapes that are wider than they are tall slide horizontally left and right, and shapes that are taller than they are wide slide vertically up and down.

▶ See the example solution to the right to understand how this works. For example, consider the 2 in the top row: it can move into 2 spaces. Meanwhile, the 0 at the bottom-right cannot move into any spaces; the spaces above it do not count because it does not slide this way.

▶ TRY IT ◀

DAY 1: EXERCISE 2

Most people have some routine to their lives, but what routines do you have? Make a note of some parts of your life that you perform in more or less the same way every time you do them:

▶ 1: _____

▶ 2: _____

▶ 3: _____

▶ 4: _____

Now think about how you could vary them in some way – whether it's to change a route, replace a favourite meal, go to a different coffee shop, go for walks in a new place, or dress in an alternative style. Whatever it is, make a brief note of what you could do to freshen up your routine, to create new experiences:

▶ 1: _____

▶ 2: _____

▶ 3: _____

▶ 4: _____

If you've written out some ideas, then you could even consider putting one (or more!) of them into practice. Your brain could thank you for it.

BRAIN TRAINING

+ Stimulate your brain with new and novel challenges
+ Teach your brain new tricks, aiding smarter thinking
+ All novelty is good – there's no magic bullet

WHAT?

Brain training is any activity which stimulates you mentally in a way that's good for your brain, encouraging it to build new connections that make you smarter. It includes the concept of 'use it or lose it', meaning that if you don't continue to challenge yourself you will lose existing mental skills. It also encompasses the idea that practising one skill can make you smarter at other skills.

WHY?

It's important to continually make good use of your brain in order to preserve what you have – and build new abilities. It doesn't matter what activities you choose, but the more they differ from your everyday life and experiences then the more benefit they are likely to have.

Suggested time to spend
12 MINUTES

FUN AND VARIED EXERCISES

Your brain doesn't learn well when it is bored or unchallenged, so a good brain-training exercise will require concentration. It also helps if the exercise is fun, since it can be hard to maintain focus when you aren't enjoying something.

Most activities become easier with practice, so even the best brain-training exercises can become less beneficial with time. Variety is always key, and once you have 'been there, done that' with an activity, you are unlikely to gain the same mental benefit. For example, while your first sudoku will be of great interest to your brain, it's unlikely that the thousandth will bring the same benefit – even if you are still enjoy the solving.

GENERAL IMPROVEMENT

Practising brain-training exercises will make you better at those specific exercises, just as practising any skill will improve your abilities at that skill. But do those same brain-training exercises *also* make you better at unrelated tasks too, or improve your general intelligence?

Recent, large-scale research studies suggest that repetitive brain-training exercises of the kind sometimes found in online games will only get you so far. There is no strong evidence that these games make you smarter at completely unrelated activities – unless, that is, you are over 50. For the over 50s, this type of brain training has been shown to lead to gains in other aspects of life. Whether this is due to brain changes with age, or if it is simply that older people inherently face fewer brain challenges in their everyday lives, remains to be seen. It makes sense that the relative improvement brought by brain training will depend on the daily level of mental challenge you face.

MEMORY GAINS

While simple brain-training games may not be a panacea for your general intelligence, one type of brain-training game that *is* worthy of more interest is those that work on your memory. Most of us now store names, numbers, addresses, birthdays, shopping lists and a whole host of other information on phones (or if not, then an address book or calendar), and we are used to looking things up online rather than having to remember them. This means that many of us don't make much deliberate use of our memory once we have finished our education.

It has been shown that brain-training tasks that work on your memory skills can lead to meaningful improvements in related memory tasks – although, as with general brain training, you would not expect to see any gain in more distantly related memory skills.

TRY IT NOW

This book features a wide range of brain-training exercises, avoiding the repetitive nature of some online games.

For each exercise, it's worth remembering that the aim is not to cause frustration. Your brain learns best when its happy and relaxed – so if a puzzle starts to make you feel stressed, then put it down and come back to it later.

You'll also find solutions to the exercises – where a solution is appropriate – at the back of the book, indexed by day and exercise number. If you're stuck on a puzzle, you could always take a look at the solution and see how it connects to the information you already had.

DAY 2: EXERCISE 1

Challenge your word skills by rearranging each of the following sets of letters to form as many words as you can. Each word must use all of the letters.

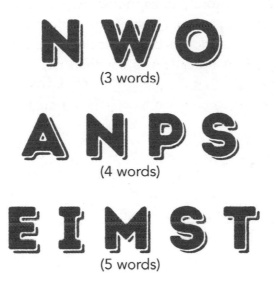

N W O
(3 words)

A N P S
(4 words)

E I M S T
(5 words)

DAY 2: EXERCISE 2

For each of the following two cubes, which of the four shape nets could be cut out and folded up to make that cube?

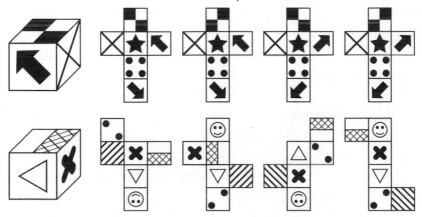

ACHIEVING FOCUS

+ Eliminate things you know may distract you
+ Focus on a single task at a time
+ Get things done by breaking into component tasks

WHAT?

You are far less capable when you are distracted, or are not adequately focusing on a task. By learning to maintain focus, you can complete tasks more quickly and to a higher standard. Spending even a small amount of time preparing to work can often save you considerable time overall.

WHY?

Being focused makes you more efficient, and in turn you have more time for other projects – or even just to relax. This leads to a sense of achievement which in turn helps reduce stress levels. This creates a pleasing sense of satisfaction and a virtuous loop, whereby you can get further things done more quickly – and all without doing them any less well.

Suggested time to spend
18 MINUTES

▶ IN DEPTH ◀

DISTRACTIONS

Distractions come from all directions. They can be audible, such as a background conversation or a ringing phone, or visual, such as an email notification or the arrival of another person. They can also be physical, such as a cold draught across your face, or even odour-related, such as the aroma of food.

It may not be possible to avoid all potential distractions, but it is often worth trying to eliminate as many as possible. Don't be afraid to ask people to leave you alone for a certain amount of time. In most circumstances it also won't cause any great harm if you're unavailable on your phone or email for an hour or so. Set up a separate way for people to contact you in a genuine emergency, if necessary.

FOCUS

To get things done, you need to try to focus on the task in hand. Eliminating likely distractions is an important part of this, but it's also necessary to avoid mental distractions such as thinking about other tasks, or wondering about some external issue.

There are many different methods designed to help you get things done, but key points are:

▶ Don't try to do two things at once. You can't consciously think about multiple things at the same time.

▶ Set yourself realistic goals, so you don't get put off by an impossible target, or work aimlessly.

▶ Split complex tasks into smaller, more manageable sub-tasks, so that you can get started on them.

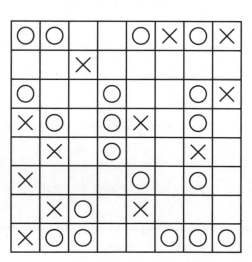

▶ TRY IT ◀

DAY 3: EXERCISE 1

Some puzzles are solved primarily by focusing and searching for the next move in an orderly fashion without getting distracted.

In this puzzle the aim is simple. Place an 'O' or an 'X' in every square, without making any lines of four or more of the same symbol in any direction, including diagonally.

▶ 1.

▶ 2.

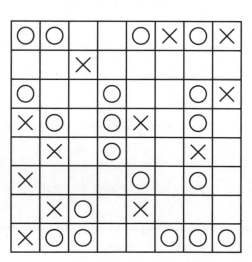

DAY 3: EXERCISE 2

This puzzle is somewhat similar, but now you must place either a '0' or a '1' into every square so that you have no more than two of the same symbol next to each other in any row or column.

Note that there are no diagonal constraints in these two puzzles – just the rows and columns.

▶ 1.

	1		0		0	0	1
	1		0		0		1
		1			1	1	
0				0	0		1
1		0	0				0
	0	1			0		
0		1		0		1	
1	1	0		1		0	

▶ 2.

	0						
		0		1	0		
1		1				0	
		1	1		1		
		0		1	1		
	0				0		0
		1	0		0		
						0	

REALISTIC TARGETS

+ What are your hopes and goals?
+ What steps can you take to make bring them closer?
+ Break down complex tasks into simpler ones

WHAT?

Most people have dreams, but if you want to achieve them then what are you doing to bring them closer? You might win the lottery, or by sheer luck bump into the person who can make your goals a reality, but depending on pure chance is not a reliable plan. So what can be done to help you achieve your goals?

WHY?

It's great to dream, but it's often even better to *do*. If there are targets you wish to reach, or goals you want to achieve, then making a realistic plan to help bring them closer to completion is a great start. And even if those goals will need elements of luck to achieve, it's good to make a plan that lets you roll the dice as many times as you can.

Suggested time to spend
12 MINUTES

STEP-BY-STEP

Every journey has to start, and sometimes taking the first step is the hardest. It might involve reaching outside your comfort zone, perhaps by speaking directly to people you would normally avoid, or by talking yourself up in a way that you wouldn't normally do. If you are setting up on your own, it might involve making sales and marketing calls that you find intimidating, or it could involve seeking honest opinions and making yourself vulnerable in a way that you don't enjoy. But whatever it is you want to achieve, start by breaking it down:

▶ What are all of the things I need to be able to do in order to achieve the goals I am aiming for?

▶ Can I do those things? Or, if not, then is there a realistic way of involving other people to help?

▶ If I have identified things I can't do, then is my original goal truly realistic or should I adjust my aims?

Being honest with yourself right from the start is important, because striving for an impossible goal can only end in wasted time and disappointment.

BREAK IT DOWN

Once you have set your sights, break out a series of tasks which will help you progress along the journey to your goal. The simpler the tasks (e.g. 'Write to a friend who can help') the better, since they become more achievable – although it is also best to avoid creating *too* many tasks so that your 'to do' list does not become completely overwhelming.

► TRY IT ◄

DAY 4: EXERCISE 1

Think of a goal you wish to achieve. Write it here:

_____

What skills and abilities will you need to achieve this goal? Do you have all of them? What are the major stumbling blocks along the way? Can you think of three?

▶ 1. _____

▶ 2. _____

▶ 3. _____

What smaller, more achievable tasks can you break this goal down into? And can each of these smaller tasks be itself broken down into further tasks? Will each of these help you on your journey towards the larger goal?

Write down some of the smaller subtasks you could aim to do:

▶ 1. _____

▶ 2. _____

▶ 3. _____

These are your initial thoughts, and they might change with time, so carry on thinking about these questions over the next twenty-four hours. It is natural for your ideas to begin to evolve once you start considering them in detail.

DAY 4: EXERCISE 2

This puzzle has a trivial aim, at least compared against life goals, but it may still require some careful thought to break it down and solve.

Look at this circle of dots:

Can you find a way to draw a perfect square whose edges travel through the centre of every one of these eight dots?

SETTING PRIORITIES

+ Rank tasks by importance and deadline
+ Remember to look out for yourself – not just others
+ Reward yourself for completing goals

WHAT?

Deciding what to do, and when, is fundamental to many aspects of life. Sometimes you have no choice in the matter, but when you are trying to achieve a specific set of goals then it's important to prioritize and focus on those that matter most.

WHY?

No matter how small or large the goal, without a clear plan and associated priorities then you might never achieve the things you want to, whether in life or in work. If the only thing standing in the way is you, then it's time to discard the excuses and make a plan to get where you want to be. A key part of this is focusing on the sequence of steps that will take you there, and ensuring you set priorities so that you work on them in the most effective order.

Suggested time to spend
15 MINUTES

IDENTIFYING PRIORITIES

Yesterday, we looked at how you can break a complex task down into smaller, more achievable tasks. But once you have that list of less complex tasks, how do you decide where to start? The simpler goals won't help if you feel overwhelmed by having 'too much to do'.

► Identify which tasks will provide the most benefit, soonest, and start with those

► Don't be afraid to change your priorities as you make progress and become more knowledgeable

► Prioritize the things that matter most to you, rather than focusing simply on those that are easiest

► Do some tasks depend on finishing others first?

Once you have decided on a priority for each task, sort them into order of decreasing priority. Now you have both a plan *and* an idea of the order in which you can tackle them.

YOUR OWN GOALS

Most of us live around other people, so our own goals need to fit in with the needs and requirements of those around us. But at the end of the day, it's important to look out for your own needs as well as those of others. Looking after yourself is an important part of looking after others. It's also important not to start to resent other people, or alternatively to blame them for your own lack of progress on your life goals. If you feel this is a problem in your life, stop and think about what you can do to improve things yourself, without relying on others to change.

▶ TRY IT ◀

COMPLETING GOALS

As you make progress towards your targets, you may find that your needs and expectations change. If so, that's great – but make sure you stop and update your plan and your priorities to adapt to the new realities.

Each time you complete one of your tasks, reward yourself in some way – even if it's just with a deep breath and a smile, it's important to acknowledge your progress. It's important to feel satisfaction when you complete a task, rather than simply the weight of all the things you might still have to do.

DAY 5: EXERCISE 1

Draw along the dashed lines to divide this grid up so as to form a complete set of dominoes, from 0-0 up to 6-6. Each domino will appear exactly once, so you can use the cross-off chart to keep track of which dominoes have been placed. Two dominoes are already placed to show how it works.

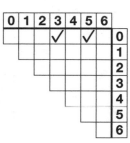

0	1	4	3	0	0	2	2
6	3	2	2	1	2	0	4
5	6	5	2	5	6	0	3
2	4	0	0	3	5	3	6
1	5	3	5	1	3	6	6
4	5	2	4	4	3	6	4
6	5	0	4	1	1	1	1

► TRY IT ◄

DAY 5: EXERCISE 2

Solve these minesweeper puzzles by locating the position of a set of mines. Mines can only be placed in empty squares, with no more than one mine per square. Numbers in the grid reveal the total number of mines in all of their touching squares, including diagonally touching squares. A small example solution is given to show how it works.

► 1.

1			2	
	4			2
	4		2	
3		3		2
				1

► 2.

		1		3		2
2	3		3			3
			4		5	
3		1				
	4			2		
		2			1	
	2				1	1

GETTING ORGANIZED

+ Things only get done when you actually start on them
+ If a task is too weighty, try to simplify it
+ Write things down so you can focus without distraction

WHAT?

Deciding to do something, and actually doing it, are sometimes very different things. For some people the main issue is getting started, as typified by 'writer's block'. For others, the main problem is maintaining focus on the original goal.

WHY?

When you are working, it's important to be actually getting things done. Otherwise, you could simply be relaxing and having fun – and so the more you are able to get things done while 'working', the more time you have left over to enjoy life. This creates a virtuous circle, whereby a happier and more relaxed you will in turn find it easier to focus and get further things done.

Suggested time to spend
15 MINUTES

▶ IN DEPTH ◀

GETTING THINGS DONE

Getting something done involves two key things:

> ▶ **Getting started, and achieving focus**

> ▶ **Maintaining that focus until the task is complete**

Most people struggle with at least one of these, so part of the secret of getting things done is being honest with yourself. What do you have trouble with, and what can you do about it?

GETTING STARTED

Getting going is often a major struggle. It's natural to push more complex tasks away in favour of simpler, easier ones, and yet unless those easier tasks have such urgency that they would be a distraction if not done, then perhaps they should wait until after. Indeed, if you were to decide they can't be begun until you complete the more complex task, this could help motivate you to get going so you can move onto them.

Some people need a deadline to get started, so if you don't have one – or it is too far away to seem 'real' – then manufacture one for yourself. And if that doesn't help, then tell a friend or family member about the deadline and ask them to hold you accountable if you miss it, perhaps by withholding a reward you might otherwise have given yourself for completing the task.

If you know you often miss deadlines, then write down every deadline, updated, so as to be days or weeks in advance of the real deadline – but then make sure you aim for the deadline you wrote down, rather than the original one.

► IN DEPTH ◄

MAINTAINING FOCUS

Perhaps there are certain times of day you work best? Maybe you work well after you've been to the gym? Or perhaps you just need a cup of tea or coffee on your desk to switch you into the right mindset? Whatever it is, each time you successfully manage to focus then have a think afterwards and see if you can identify what it was that helped you stay focused. Make a note of it, and try doing it deliberately next time.

Once you have begun, and have that initial focus which has allowed you to get going, how do you *keep* going? Maintaining focus requires you to minimize distractions before you begin, but just as importantly it involves avoiding *mental* distractions of your own creation once you have started. One simple idea that helps most people is a relatively easy thing to do:

► **Write things down**

It's an unpleasant feeling to be keeping in your head a list of things you are meaning to do, thoughts you want to explore, or tasks you have to complete. So don't – write them down. Dumping out your brain to paper can let you focus on the most immediate task in hand, rather than being distracted by thoughts of other things to do.

TIMING TASKS

In advance of trying a task, estimate how long it will take you – and write this down. Set aside enough time to complete it, so you don't get interrupted by other deadlines. And if your estimate turns out be wrong, then use your experience to try and write more realistic estimates for future tasks.

DAY 6: EXERCISE 1

For each of these two fences puzzles, draw horizontal and vertical lines to join all of the dots together to form one loop which visits every dot.

▶ 1.

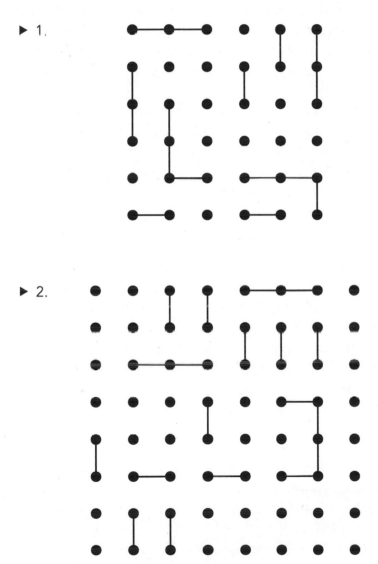

▶ 2.

DEALING WITH STRESS

+ Your brain behaves differently when stressed
+ A small amount of stress can be helpful
+ Continued or chronic stress must be dealt with

WHAT?

Everyone experiences stress from time to time. It's part of being human, as an evolutionary response to moments of heightened danger. Your body is on edge, ready to react quickly to an immediate threat. This can be helpful for short periods of time.

WHY?

Small amounts of stress can prime you for action, helping you to focus on a task and get it done. But stress can be unpleasant, both to you and to those you have to deal with while stressed! Long-term stress, however, leads to negative changes in the brain, and so sources of chronic stress must be addressed and removed, wherever possible.

Suggested time to spend
25 MINUTES

REDUCING STRESS

Intermittent stresses can be dealt with in various ways, including:

> ▶ Humour – laughter is proven to alleviate stress

> ▶ Physical exercise – the more strenuous the better, although *any* exercise will help

> ▶ Social contact – a feeling of connectedness, or of having shared a problem, can help significantly

> ▶ Setting aside time for relaxation – assign times where you know in advance you won't be working on, or thinking about, stressful issues

Even better, you could try removing the source of the stress itself, if you know what it is and are able to do so. If it's a piece of work that is waiting to be completed, then at least you can look forward to having finished it in the future.

SLOW DOWN

Although stress is often caused by things that are yet to be done, somewhat counter-intuitively it can actually help to slow down to reduce stress. The stress itself can lead to you feeling that you must rush, which perpetuates the problem.

Give yourself a realistic amount of time to complete a task, or divide the time remaining into realistic sub-goals, and so long as you are keeping to the timetable then you have no reason to feel stressed. Stress is a biological call to action, and so you need to convince your brain that there is no immediate urgent situation.

▶ TRY IT ◀

DAY 7: EXERCISE 1

Colour this image with these colours to reveal a hidden picture:

1 = light blue	4 = white	7 = orange	A = brown
2 = blue	5 = green	8 = red	B = light brown
3 = dark blue	6 = yellow	9 = dark red	

► TRY IT ◄

DAY 7: EXERCISE 2

Try completing this dot-to-dot puzzle to reveal a cuddly friend.

Start at '1', marked by a solid star, and draw a line to '2', then draw a line to '3' and so on until you reach another star (which will be hollow). Then lift your pen or pencil and find the next number, which is again marked with a solid star. Continue joining lines in the same way until all the dots have been used.

THE POWER OF SLEEP

+ The human body needs sleep to survive
+ Your brain remains extremely busy as you sleep
+ Long-term memories are secured during sleep

WHAT?

Without sleep you will die. After about ten days without sleep, your body will have had enough. But long before that, after about eighteen or so hours without sleep, your judgement will start to become impaired. Many important biological processes take place during sleep, not least in your brain.

WHY?

The full details of sleep remain a mystery to us, but we know it is crucial for cementing long-term memories. During sleep, your brain processes the events of the day, consolidating information it has learned and making sense of it. Your brain also continues to think, even though you are not conscious of it, which is why you may sometimes wake up with a new idea to tackle a problem you have been facing.

Suggested time to spend
15 MINUTES

▶ IN DEPTH ◀

GO TO BED

Some people are terrible at going to sleep. They go to bed late, then wake up feeling awful. This is not good for your brain, and it's not good for the rest of your body either.

Fix a time you plan to go to bed, and do everything you can to stick to it. Sometimes life will interfere, but staying up late for leisure, such as reading social media or playing games, is not sensible. It's better to wake up early and do these, when you will still have the option of extra sleep should you need it, rather than stay up late.

SEVEN HOURS+

Almost everyone needs seven hours of sleep or more, although some of us can get by with just six hours. There are very few who cope well on less than that – although some people get used to the effects of tiredness and kid themselves that they can do so. Young children and the elderly have different requirements, however.

TROUBLE SLEEPING

If you regularly have trouble sleeping, it's important to fix this as soon as you can. If you know what is disturbing you, such as a noise or even a source of stress, try to sort out the source of that disturbance. Or if you don't know why, or are unable to resolve it yourself, then speak to a GP. Keep a sleep diary so that they can assess you and see how significant the problem is (or, hopefully, isn't). Lack of sleep can lead to a wide range of mental problems, and make you a danger both to yourself and to others – and it is an unpleasant way to live your life.

▶ TRY IT ◀

DAY 8: EXERCISE 1

If you can't immediately solve them, try sleeping on these riddles and see if inspiration strikes while you're asleep!

▶ There is something which I can add to any box – even one which doesn't close – to make it permanently lighter. What is it?

▶ What is it that goes up whenever you come down with it?

▶ What can be stuck in just one place and yet is still able to travel the world?

▶ You're in a race and you overtake the person in second place. What position are you now in?

▶ The more there is of it, the harder it is to see. What is it?

▶ What can you run out of, and yet it will last forever?

▶ How can you throw a ball with all your might and yet still guarantee it will come straight back to you?

▶ From what five-letter word can you remove two letters and yet only have one left?

▶ When can you add five to nine and end up with two as the answer?

▶ What gets larger whenever you take something away from it?

DAY 8: EXERCISE 2

Decode these famous quotes by shifting each letter up or down the alphabet by a constant amount. Wrap around from Z to A and vice-versa. For example, if the shift was '+3' then you would change A to D, change B to E, and so on until you changed X to A, changed Y to B and changed Z to C.

▶ UIFSF JT OPUIJOH FJUIFS HPPE
PS CBE CVU UIJOLJOH NBLFT JU TP

▶ NK RZXNH GJ YMJ KTTI
TK QTAJ, UQFD TS

▶ MLC RMSAF MD LYRSPC
KYICQ RFC UFMJC UMPJB IGL

▶ WUBCFOBQS WG HVS QIFGS CT
UCR; YBCKZSRUS WG HVS KWBU
KVSFSKWHV KS TZM HC VSOJSB

▶ EZ MP, ZC YZE EZ MP,
ESLE TD ESP BFPDETZY

BODY AND BRAIN

+ Physical fitness goes hand in hand with mental health
+ Your brain needs a regular supply of certain chemicals
+ The fitter you are, the faster you can think

WHAT?

Your brain needs a constant supply of certain chemicals in order to function well. Physical fitness and a balanced diet are necessary to provide these chemicals in order to maintain and protect your brain.

WHY?

Each brain cell inside your brain can only store a small amount of energy, so needs a steady supply of oxygen to carry on activating. If you aren't fit enough, your brain will need to wait longer for its energy to be replenished before you can use that thinking pathway again. You also need to consume a balanced diet so your brain has the vitamins, minerals and essential fatty acids it requires to function well.

Suggested time to spend
15 MINUTES

EXERCISE EVERY DAY

If staying physically fit isn't a good enough reason to exercise every day – even if it's just a brisk walk – then looking after your brain surely is. We now know that aerobic exercise is essential in order to keep your brain healthy:

> ▶ Exercise stimulates physical improvements in your brain

> ▶ Exercise helps you learn

> ▶ Exercise makes it easier to concentrate afterwards

> ▶ Exercise can reduce stress and to a certain degree help alleviate depression

> ▶ Exercise can help you come up with creative ideas

In fact, exercise is so important that there is significant and compelling evidence to prove that:

> ▶ Exercise helps counteract the natural death of brain cells, helping slow the onset of dementia in the elderly

START NOW

It's never too late to start. If you have sat in a chair all day, then get up and walk around for a bit. If you don't exercise regularly, work out how you can fit aerobic exercise into your schedule – it could be as simple as walking just part of a regular journey. Anything is better than nothing, although more exercise is generally better than less – up to a sensible limit, at least.

A HEALTHY DIET

Your brain *needs* certain chemicals to work. Oxygen is the most immediate demand, of course, but a balanced diet is a key part of looking after your brain, which must include:

▶ Vitamins – organic compounds your body can't make itself
▶ Minerals – chemical elements your body needs
▶ Essential fatty acids – including omega-3 polyunsaturated fatty acids
▶ Essential amino acids – these are found in proteins

A healthy diet can be summed up quite simply:

▶ **Eat a balanced and varied range of food, without excessive consumption – and avoid fad diets**

Other tips recommended by medical professionals include:

▶ **Eat breakfast**

▶ **Use a smaller plate, so it doesn't look empty**

▶ **Eat more slowly, so you have a chance to feel full**

▶ **Drink more water**

OMEGA-3

Omega-3 fatty acids are essential for the good operation of your brain, but there is no evidence that consumption beyond the recommended daily allowance (RDA) will make you any smarter. There is, however, evidence that dietary supplement pills of these are far less effective – so eat actual fish, or other sources such as linseed, instead of relying on supplements.

► TRY IT ◄

DAY 9: EXERCISE 1

Write a number into every empty square so that the top grid contains the numbers 1 to 36 once each, and the bottom grid contains the numbers 1 to 64 once each. Place the numbers so that they form a path from 1 to the final number, moving left/right/up/down between squares. At each step of the path the value in the square must increase by exactly 1.

► 1.

	32			35	
30					19
	23	16			
	24	15			
7					12
	5			2	

► 2.

		5			62		
	17		1	60		64	
		19			34		
		20			35		
	14		30	37		47	
		22			39		

CHANGE YOUR BRAIN

+ Your brain learns throughout your entire life
+ You can grow new brain cells in some areas of the brain
+ Your brain is continually changing and evolving

WHAT?

Your brain can build and reorganize connections throughout your life, allowing it to learn new ways of thinking. It can even make new brain cells, at least in some parts of your brain – such as those associated with long-term memory.

WHY?

The brain changes rapidly and significantly in early life – and once upon a time we thought that was it. But the truth is that in adulthood your brain continues to reorganize itself, at least on a small scale, in order to best fit to your life. Unused parts can be discarded, and new connections can be built. In the case of traumatic injury, it can even undergo more significant rewiring to allow lost skills to be rebuilt in undamaged areas of the brain.

Suggested time to spend
30 MINUTES

DAY 10: EXERCISE 1

Place a letter from A to H into each empty square, so that no letter repeats in any row or column. Additionally, two identical letters cannot touch – not even diagonally.

► 1.

F		B	D		A
	C			B	
D					C
A					B
	D			F	
C		E	B		F

► 2.

A	C					H	F
B			E	F			A
		A			F		
	F		A	C		E	
	H		G	B		A	
		D			B		
H			C	D			G
C	A					G	E

DAY 10: EXERCISE 2

Write a number into every empty square so that the top grid contains the numbers 1 to 36 once each, and the bottom grid contains the numbers 1 to 64 once each. Place the numbers so that they form a path from 1 to the final number, moving between touching squares in any direction, including diagonally. At each step of the path the value in the square must increase by exactly 1.

► 1.

13	15	17			
	14		33		36
					31
	8	1	21		30
		23	22	25	
		3			26

► 2.

		57		15	16		
	28						
31				55		10	
32		64				19	9
	25			53	20		7
					1	6	
	37		47	42	45		
		38	41				3

▶ TRY IT ◀

DAY 10: EXERCISE 3

Write a number from 0 to 9 into every empty box so that:

▶ Each column adds up to the total in the grey box
▶ Each row contains the digits 0 to 9 once each
▶ Identical digits aren't in touching squares – not even diagonally

▶ 1.

	7		2				0		
	9	0	5		2		1	6	8
	7	8			6	4		2	3
	6		7	2		1			
		0	5	1			2		3
19	37	17	20	24	23	21	16	27	21

▶ 2.

2		1					6	7	
	9	6				5			
8				4	6	0			3
			6		2	1		8	0
	8	7	2				5	9	6
15	38	21	25	22	20	6	25	33	20

CHALLENGE YOURSELF

+ Your brain loves to learn
+ Try new things, and aim to acquire new skills
+ Don't get stuck in an unchanging routine

WHAT?

Look for new and novel tasks so as to more fully engage your brain. The more out-of-the-ordinary an activity it is, the more your brain has to pay attention and think – and learn. Regular parts of life start to be handled on 'autopilot' by your brain, so break out of the rut and try something new.

WHY?

Your brain is incredibly powerful, and it likes to make life as easy as possible for you by saving you from having to consciously think about the mundanities of life. The flip side of this, however, is that you may need to try something new to really challenge your brain. These new challenges will encourage your brain to preserve your existing skills, and help it build new ways of thinking so as to better tackle further challenges.

Suggested time to spend
20 MINUTES

► TRY IT ◄

DAY 11: EXERCISE 1

Next time you're out and about somewhere familiar, try looking up. What do you see? The world above street level is often a curiously unseen place, with architecture that most of us never notice.

It's also worth stopping to truly look at things you see every day and yet never pay much attention to. Particularly if you regularly drive past something, stopping and walking past it instead can be a surprisingly different experience.

And if you really want to take this exercise to the next level, then take every chance you can to travel to new places. Your brain has to work really hard in unfamiliar locations, because there's so much to process and understand. The further from home, the better.

DAY 11: EXERCISE 2

Try these word riddles, to get your brain thinking in unusual ways. In each case, the answer involves a play on words.

> ► What occurs once in a minute, twice
> in a moment, but never in a year?

> ► We all know that one comes before two, but when
> do three, four and five also all come before two?

> ► What word becomes shorter when
> you add more letters to it?

> ► Why is the letter 'A' like noon?

► TRY IT ◄

DAY 11: EXERCISE 3

Solve this kakuro puzzle by placing a digit from 1 to 9 into every empty white square. Each horizontal run of white cells must add up to the total above the diagonal line to the left of the run, and each vertical run of white cells must add up to the total below the diagonal line above the run. No digit can be used more than once in any run.

DAY 11: EXERCISE 4

Place a number from 1 to 5 in every square, to represent a building of one of that number of storeys, so that every row and column within the grid contains one of each number.

▶ Numbers outside the grid reveal the number of visible buildings, looking into the grid from that point along the touching row or column.

▶ Taller buildings block the view of all shorter buildings that are further away. For example, a row containing 32451 would have a clue of '3' to its left, since the 3, 4 and 5 are visible, and a clue of '2' to its right, since only the 1 and 5 are visible.

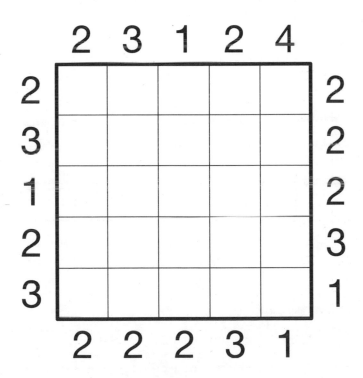

DAY 12 RELAXATION

+ It's important to take a break from time to time
+ Do something very different when taking a break
+ Set aside time to relax

WHAT?

It's important to take breaks, particularly after a period of extended intense focus. These breaks need not be very long, but it's good to give yourself a chance to recover from moments of intense thought.

WHY?

Scheduling breaks makes work more bearable. It gives your brain a chance to process what you've just been doing, and it's good to have a plan to take breaks so you can aim to complete certain tasks in advance of them – and then have a small reward for doing so. When taking a break, try to switch your focus to something very different – so if you have been studying a book then take a walk or listen to some music; or if you have been working on a computer, perhaps stop and read a physical book.

Suggested time to spend
15 MINUTES

DAY 12: EXERCISE 1

Try the following relaxing puzzles during your next break.

Start by completing this dot-to-dot puzzle to reveal some wintery pals. Begin at '1', marked by a solid star, and draw a line to '2', then draw a line to '3' and so on until you reach another star (which will be hollow). Then lift your pen or pencil and find the next number, which is again marked with a solid star. Continue joining lines in the same way until all the dots have been used.

▶ TRY IT ◀

DAY 12: EXERCISE 2

Find your way through this maze, from top to bottom.

DAY 12: EXERCISE 3

How many words can you find in each of these word circles? Each word must use the central letter plus two or more other letters. There is one word in each circle that uses all the letters.

▶ 1.

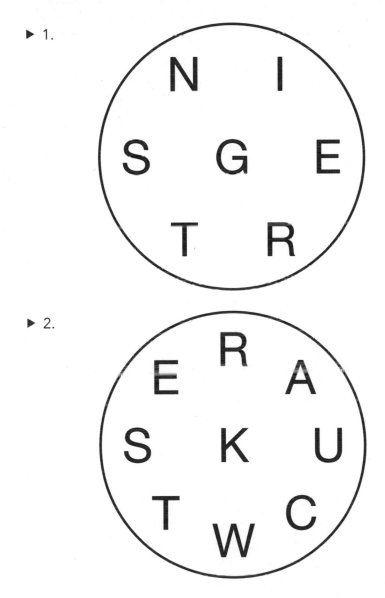

▶ 2.

DAY 13 MINDFUL MEDITATION

+ Rest doesn't have to be just while you sleep
+ Taking a moment to not think about anything can help
+ Mindfulness comes in many forms

WHAT?

Mindfulness techniques involve meditating by focusing purely on your breathing, and considering any other thoughts that enter your mind as distractions that you can observe and then dismiss. Prayer can also be a form of mindfulness.

WHY?

Some people find meditation or other mindfulness techniques to be helpful in dealing with stress or related problems. Having a reliable method of temporarily freeing yourself from whatever burdens or desires you might currently be carrying can help relieve these symptoms. It can, for example, help you feel in control of your life, by giving you an ability to manage the maelstrom of thoughts that might otherwise be swirling around your brain.

Suggested time to spend
20 MINUTES

► TRY IT ◄

MINDFULNESS

You can try the basics of mindfulness simply by sitting quietly, somewhere you will not be disturbed for a few minutes. Then close your eyes and pay attention to your breathing. Let your anxieties and other thoughts gently float away, until all you are aware of is your physical presence in the current moment.

You can also use mindfulness as a technique to help you get to sleep. It can be particularly effective if you find yourself unable to let go of thoughts from the day that is ending, or worries for the days that are to follow.

As you tackle the following exercises, try to clear your mind and think about nothing other than the individual puzzles.

DAY 13: EXERCISE 1

Try this simple creativity task in which there are no right or wrong answers. Just join some of all of the dots in any way that you please. As you go, you might even find a picture emerging.

► TRY IT ◄

DAY 13: EXERCISE 2

Find your way through this maze, from top to bottom.

DAY 13: EXERCISE 3

Colour each square according to the key to reveal a picture.

```
1 1 1 1 1 1 1 1 1 1 1 1 2 1 1 1 1 1 1 1 1 1 1 1 1 1 2 2 2 2 2 2
1 1 1 1 1 1 1 1 1 1 1 1 2 2 2 2 1 1 1 1 1 1 1 1 1 1 2 2 2 2 2 2
1 1 1 1 1 1 1 1 1 1 1 2 2 2 2 2 1 1 1 1 2 1 1 1 1 1 2 2 2 2 2 2
1 1 1 1 1 1 1 1 1 2 2 2 2 2 2 2 1 2 2 2 2 1 1 1 1 1 2 2 2 2 2 2
1 1 1 1 1 1 1 1 1 3 3 2 2 2 2 2 2 2 2 2 2 1 1 1 1 1 1 1 2 2 2 2
1 1 1 1 1 1 1 1 1 1 3 3 3 3 3 3 3 3 3 3 1 1 1 1 1 1 1 1 1 1 1 1
1 1 1 1 1 1 1 2 2 2 2 2 4 4 4 4 4 4 2 2 2 2 1 1 1 1 1 1 1 1 1 1
1 1 1 1 1 1 1 2 2 2 2 4 4 4 4 4 4 4 2 2 2 1 1 1 1 1 1 1 1 1 1 1
1 1 1 1 1 1 1 2 2 2 2 4 4 5 5 5 5 4 4 2 2 2 2 2 1 1 1 1 1 1 1 1
1 1 1 1 1 1 1 3 2 2 4 4 5 5 5 5 4 4 2 2 2 2 2 1 1 1 1 1 1 1 1 1
1 1 1 1 1 1 1 3 3 4 4 5 5 5 5 5 4 4 3 3 2 2 2 1 1 1 1 1 1 1 1 1
1 1 1 1 1 1 1 3 3 4 4 5 5 5 5 5 4 4 2 3 2 2 2 1 1 1 1 1 1 1 1 6
1 1 1 1 1 1 1 2 2 2 2 4 4 4 4 4 4 2 1 3 1 1 1 1 1 1 1 1 6 6 6 6
1 1 1 1 1 1 1 2 2 2 2 3 4 4 4 4 4 2 2 1 1 1 1 1 1 1 6 6 6 6 6 6
1 1 1 1 1 1 1 2 2 3 3 2 2 2 2 3 3 2 2 2 2 1 1 1 1 6 6 6 6 6 6 6
7 7 7 7 7 7 2 2 3 3 7 2 2 2 3 3 2 2 2 2 7 7 7 7 7 7 7 7 7 7 7 7
7 7 7 7 7 7 7 2 2 2 7 2 2 2 3 8 3 2 2 2 7 7 7 7 7 7 7 7 7 7 7 7
7 7 7 7 7 7 7 7 7 7 2 2 2 3 8 8 3 3 7 7 7 7 7 7 7 7 7 7 7 7 7 7
7 7 7 7 7 7 7 7 7 7 2 2 3 3 8 8 8 7 7 7 7 7 7 7 7 7 7 7 7 7 7 7
7 7 7 7 7 7 7 7 7 7 7 7 7 8 8 8 7 7 7 7 7 7 7 7 7 7 7 7 7 7 7 7
7 7 7 7 9 9 9 9 7 7 7 7 7 8 8 8 7 7 7 7 7 7 7 7 9 9 9 9 7 7 7 7
2 2 2 2 9 9 9 9 9 9 9 2 2 8 8 8 2 2 2 2 9 9 9 9 9 9 9 9 2 2 2 2
2 2 2 2 9 9 9 9 9 9 9 9 9 8 8 8 2 2 9 9 9 9 9 9 9 9 2 2 2 2 2 2
6 6 6 2 2 2 9 9 9 9 9 9 9 8 8 8 2 0 0 0 0 0 9 6 6 6 6 0 0 2 2 2
6 6 6 6 6 6 6 9 9 9 9 9 9 8 8 8 2 9 9 9 9 9 6 6 6 6 6 6 6 6 6 6
6 6 6 6 6 6 6 6 6 9 9 9 9 8 8 8 9 9 9 9 9 6 6 6 6 6 6 6 6 6 6 6
6 6 6 6 6 6 6 6 6 6 6 8 8 8 8 8 9 9 9 8 6 6 6 6 6 6 6 6 6 6 6 6
6 6 6 6 6 6 6 6 6 6 6 6 8 8 8 8 9 9 8 6 6 6 6 6 6 6 6 6 6 6 6 6
9 6 6 6 6 6 6 6 6 6 6 6 6 8 8 8 8 8 6 6 6 6 6 6 6 6 6 6 6 6 6 9
9 9 6 6 6 6 6 6 6 6 6 6 6 8 8 8 8 8 6 6 6 6 6 6 6 6 6 6 9 9 9 9
9 9 9 6 6 6 0 0 0 0 0 0 0 0 0 0 0 0 0 0 0 0 0 0 9 9 9 9 9 9 9 9
9 9 9 9 9 9 0 0 0 0 0 0 0 0 0 0 0 0 0 0 0 0 9 9 9 9 9 9 9 9 9 9
9 9 8 8 9 9 9 9 5 5 5 5 5 5 5 5 5 5 5 5 9 9 9 9 9 9 9 9 9 9 9 9
9 9 8 8 8 9 9 9 5 5 5 5 5 5 5 5 5 5 5 5 9 9 9 9 9 9 9 9 9 9 9 9
8 8 8 8 8 8 9 9 5 5 5 5 5 5 5 5 5 5 5 5 9 9 9 9 9 9 9 9 8 8 8 8
8 8 8 8 8 8 9 9 0 0 0 0 0 0 0 0 0 0 0 0 9 9 8 8 8 8 8 8 8 8 8 8
8 8 8 8 8 8 8 0 0 0 0 0 0 0 0 0 0 0 0 0 0 8 8 8 8 8 8 8 8 8 8 8
8 8 8 8 8 8 8 0 0 0 0 0 0 0 0 0 0 0 0 0 0 8 8 8 8 8 8 8 8 8 8 8
8 8 8 8 8 8 8 0 0 0 0 0 0 0 0 0 0 0 0 0 0 8 8 8 8 8 8 8 8 8 8 8
8 8 8 8 8 8 8 8 8 8 5 5 5 5 5 5 5 5 5 5 8 8 8 8 8 8 8 8 8 8 8 8
8 8 8 8 8 8 8 8 8 8 5 5 5 5 5 5 5 5 5 5 8 8 8 8 8 8 8 8 8 8 8 8
```

0 = red; 1 = light blue; 2 = yellow; 3 = dark yellow; 4 = orange;
5 = dark red; 6 = brown; 7 = blue; 8 = dark green; 9 = green

BEING CREATIVE

+ Some people think that they aren't 'creative'
+ But you are continually creatively solving problems
+ You can harness your creativity to help you relax

WHAT?

Every time you solve a problem, no matter how small, then unless you followed a tightly prescribed set of rules you have thought creatively to find that solution. Creativity isn't just about the arts, but you can certainly harness your innate creativity to *create* art. And what is art itself, but anything you wish it to be?

WHY?

Most people can think of at least one creative activity they think they 'can't do'. But creativity and art are in the eyes of the beholder, so who is to judge this? In truth, your brain is capable of hugely creative leaps, and harnessing this creativity can help you feel freer and more relaxed as a person. Don't let early experiences, or the opinion of others, restrict what you feel able to do.

Suggested time to spend
15 MINUTES

▶ TRY IT ◀

DAY 14: EXERCISE 1

Try these creative tasks which are all designed to give free run to your inner artist. There is no 'right' or 'wrong' answer to these.

What do you think is inside each of these four white boxes? Draw on each empty white square to reveal what is hidden within!

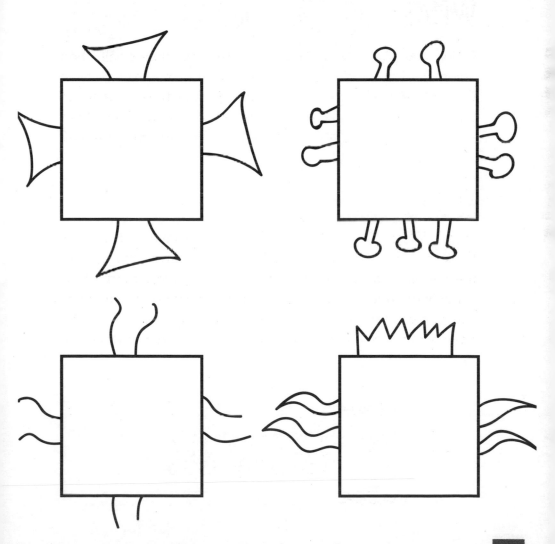

► TRY IT ◄

DAY 14: EXERCISE 2

Try creating a simple 'pixel' picture by colouring in some or all of the squares in this grid. There's no need to colour every square, and you could shade them in pencil instead of colouring, if you prefer.

Here are some ideas to get you going:

▶ TRY IT ◀

DAY 14: EXERCISE 3

Colour in the regions formed by these overlapping circles in whatever pattern or design you like. It could, for example, be a symmetrical pattern or a crazy layout of bright colours. It's entirely up to you.

BREAKING ROUTINES

+ Life shouldn't be run on rails
+ Mix up and vary parts of your life that are now routine
+ Challenge yourself with new activities

WHAT?

The older you get, the more stuck in your ways you may get. No matter your age, is there some part of your life that has become so routine that you can do it without even consciously thinking about it? Do you ever find yourself being unsure whether you've actually done something, such as made a drink or brushed your teeth?

WHY?

If you do something enough times, your clever brain learns to do it for you so you don't have to consciously think about it. In one sense this can make life simpler, but if too much of your life starts to become routine then your brain will not receive the challenges it needs.

Suggested time to spend
20 MINUTES

► TRY IT ◄

MIX IT UP

Do you always follow the same routes to and from the same small set of places? If it's safe to do so, try varying those routes. Go a longer way, or travel using a different method – for example, by bus instead of train, or by foot instead of vehicle.

If you always visit the same locations, try visiting new ones. Go shopping in a new town, go on holiday to a new location, or eat in a different restaurant. If you have a favourite drink, try a different variety or different way of making it. Try new foods, and new cuisines.

The more novelty there is in your life, the more your brain has to pay attention and the more you have to think. Lesser used circuitry in your brain can be discarded (perhaps in order to save energy), so if you don't use it then you really may lose it.

DAY 15: EXERCISE 1

Identify two things you do each time that you tend to always do in the same way, and which you can do without having to pay complete concentration all the way through:

► 1: _____

► 2: _____

Now think of a simple method to mix these up in some way:

► 1: _____

► 2: _____

DAY 15: EXERCISE 2

These hitori puzzles are a little like a sudoku puzzle in reverse. The aim is to shade in some squares so that no unshaded number appears more than once in any row or column. Also, shaded squares cannot touch, except diagonally. All unshaded squares must form a single connected area, so you can travel from any unshaded square to any other simply by moving left/right/up/down between unshaded squares.

▶ 1.

5	2	4	2	6	2
6	3	6	4	6	1
4	6	2	3	1	5
5	1	5	6	5	3
1	6	6	3	4	2
2	4	3	1	3	6

▶ 2.

7	8	3	7	4	1	6	2
4	6	8	2	5	3	7	3
6	2	7	1	3	8	2	5
2	4	6	4	8	4	1	4
1	8	2	6	3	7	2	3
5	4	1	4	2	2	8	6
1	5	2	7	6	1	4	3
8	3	1	5	6	6	2	7

DAY 15: EXERCISE 3

If you've ever played the game of battleships, try this version for a single player. The aim is to place the full set of listed ships into the grid, while obeying the rules below. An example solved puzzle is shown to the right to help make the rules clear.

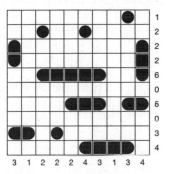

▶ Ships can't touch, not even diagonally
▶ Each row and column has a clue number showing the number of squares in that row or column that contain a ship segment
▶ Some ship segments are already given

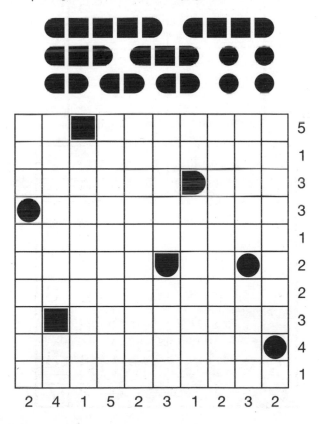

FAILURE AND REGRET

+ As you age, it is natural to accumulate regrets
+ Failure is often a matter of perception
+ Make sure your brain learns the right lessons

WHAT?

Do you ever find yourself obsessing or getting upset about things you can no longer change, or perhaps *never* had the chance to influence? If so, learn the lessons you can from those events and then move on. Living in the past will damage you in the present.

WHY?

Letting go and moving on can be difficult, but your life should be defined by more than just a few past moments or episodes. Don't worry about things you can't change, and don't spend your life waiting for other people to change – they may never do so. You owe it to your brain to get on with your life. An unhappy brain does not learn the right lessons.

Suggested time to spend
20 MINUTES

LIFE LESSONS

It's sometimes said that what doesn't kill you will only make you stronger. This may not always be true, but so often when something goes wrong in life it's tempting to think back and regret decisions you previously made. But here's the thing: you can't change them. All you can do is learn from them, and then move on. You might be upset for a while, but at some point you need to let it go so you can carry on with the rest of your life. Easy to say, perhaps, and harder to do – but necessary all the same.

Traumatic or emotional moments naturally become seared into your memory. The heightened feelings told your brain that these were important moments to remember, but the truth might be that they are moments you'd rather forget. Luckily, you can help a memory fade simply by not thinking about it. So consciously let it go, and one day it may really be gone – or so distant a memory that it no longer troubles you.

WRITE YOUR OWN HISTORY

History is, famously, written by the victors – so don't let other people's judgements impact on your own self-esteem. It's good to listen to other people's opinions and see what you can learn from them, but then form your own judgements even so. Look for the positive in everything, and you (and your brain) will be happier for it.

BE THE CHANGE YOU WANT

Don't wait for others to change. Forgive, but not necessarily forget, arguments with friends and family. Moving on is not admitting fault, but simply a sensible process of living your life.

DAY 16: EXERCISE 1

Instead of thinking futilely about past regrets, try these puzzles to help take you away from any cares of your day-to-day life!

In this hanjie puzzle, the aim is to reveal a hidden image. Shade in squares in the grid according to the clues:

▶ Numbers at the start of each row or column reveal, in order from left to right or top to bottom, the length of each consecutive run of shaded squares.
▶ There must be a gap of at least one empty square between each run of shaded squares in the same row or column.

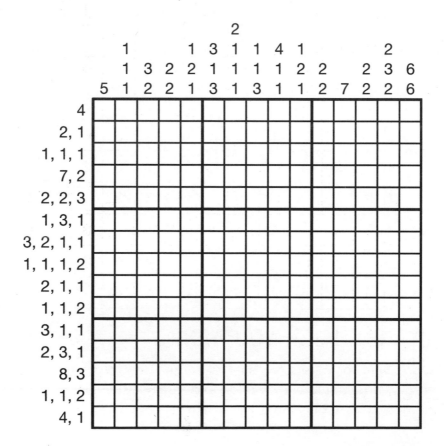

▶ TRY IT ◀

DAY 16: EXERCISE 2

In this minesweeper-type puzzle, the aim is to shade in some of the squares in order to reveal a simple hidden picture. Unlike in a regular minesweeper, you *can* shade squares with numbers in.

Each number reveals how many of the touching squares are shaded, including both diagonally touching squares *and the square itself* – so the maximum possible clue value is 9. Even when shaded, the clue number must still be obeyed.

	1		3		4	4			1
1	2		4		7	6	5		
2		5		6		5			2
2		5					6	3	2
	3			5	5			3	
	2	4		6		5		3	2
2			3	4		4	3	3	
3	4		4		4	5			3
	5	6		6	5		4	5	3
1		5		5	4	5	4	4	

KNOW YOUR STRENGTHS

+ The person who knows you best is... you
+ Identify your strengths and recognize your weaknesses
+ Don't let others tell you what you think

WHAT?

No one else is privy to your inner thoughts and desires, so by all means listen to other people's advice but ultimately try to form your own conclusions on matters where you know you know best.

WHY?

Other people may be much wiser about science, about politics, about economics, or indeed about any general subject – but you are the expert on *you*. So when it comes to making decisions that affect you directly, make sure it is you who are making them. Don't be unduly swayed by those who are simply second-guessing you. They are unlikely to think in exactly the same way that you do.

Suggested time to spend
20 MINUTES

▶ IN DEPTH ◀

MAKING DECISIONS

Difficult decisions are... well, difficult. It can be helpful to talk to other people about them and take in varying points of view, but ultimately your decisions should be *yours*. You know yourself best, and arguably it's unfair to place the burden of your choices on the shoulders of others – particularly if those decisions don't turn out as hoped, and blame is given. Conversely, you shouldn't let other people bully you (whether intentionally or not) into making decisions you would not otherwise have made, if those decisions don't also affect them.

PESSIMISM

Other people may underestimate what you are capable of, so know your strengths and don't let other people talk you out of things you know you can do. This doesn't mean being reckless, but simply believing in yourself and understanding that other people's opinions, even if sincerely expressed, may not be appropriate for you.

EXCESSIVE OPTIMISM

It's said that everyone needs to be at least a little bit optimistic in order to enjoy life, and while that is itself an incredibly pessimistic thought, it nonetheless nicely encapsulates the fact that there's nothing wrong with being optimistic when making decisions. In fact, it's a good thing – you definitely don't want to set yourself up for guaranteed failure!

Optimism, however, should be tempered with a gentle dose of reality. Don't justify a ridiculous decision to yourself with a hugely improbable chain of 'hopefully's, especially if that decision will impact on others.

DAY 17: EXERCISE 1

You'll need to take some decisions to solve these puzzles – but luckily they won't affect anything other than whether you solve them or not!

By drawing along the existing lines, can you divide each of these two shapes up into 4 identical jigsaw pieces, with no pieces left over? The pieces may be rotated versions of one another, but you cannot mirror or 'turn over' any of the pieces.

▶ 1.

▶ 2.

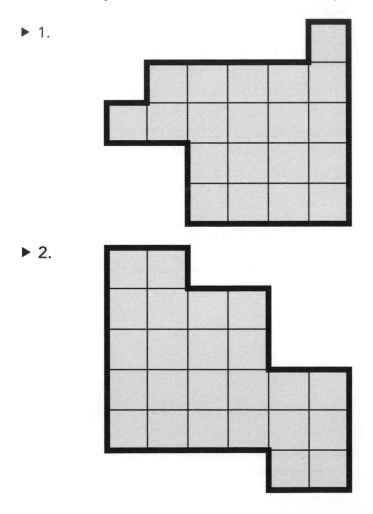

DAY 17: EXERCISE 2

Each of the following pairs of words can be linked by a third word. This third word can be added to the end of the first word, and to the start of the second word, to form two new words. Can you discover all seven link words?

WORK ____ WELL

COME ____ STREAM

KING _____ MAN

DON ___ WORD

BACK ____ AGE

HAY ____ TAP

REIN _____ WIDE

DAY 18 SELF-CONFIDENCE

+ Other people pay less attention to you than you think
+ People overstate their own confidence and success
+ Don't be excessively defensive about yourself

WHAT?

Many people suffer from feelings of inadequacy, where they either worry excessively about what people think of them, or they worry about not being as 'good' as other people.

WHY?

When you board a crowded train, walk through a packed auditorium, or even when you arrive at a bus stop full of people waiting, it's hard not to be convinced that every last person is staring at you and quite possibly judging you. But they're not. Most people are far too concerned with their own lives to pay much attention to yours. In the best possible way, you're not as interesting as you think. And similarly, other peoples' lives are a lot less interesting than they'd like you to think, too.

Suggested time to spend
20 MINUTES

DAY 18: EXERCISE 1

Unless someone has a particular reason to pay attention to you then the chances are that you barely register with them at all. See how easy it is to hide in plain sight by searching for the star, shown to the right, in this picture. Its shape is identical, although it may be drawn at a different size and rotation.

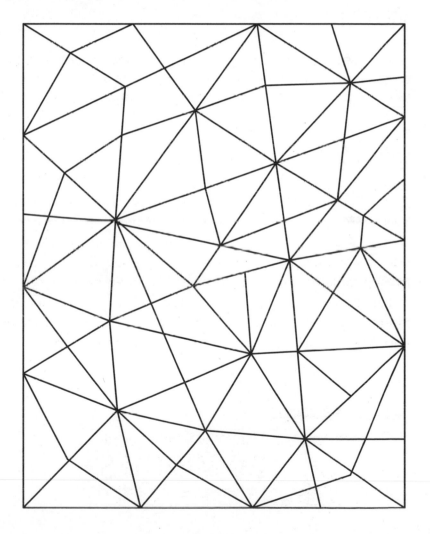

DAY 18: EXERCISE 2

See if you can build your confidence by solving these puzzles.

Complete each of these futoshiki puzzles by placing a digit from 1 to 5 in each empty box so that every number appears once in each row and column. You must also place digits so that the inequality signs between some pairs of squares are obeyed. The arrow always points at the lower of the two digits.

▶ 1.

▶ 2.

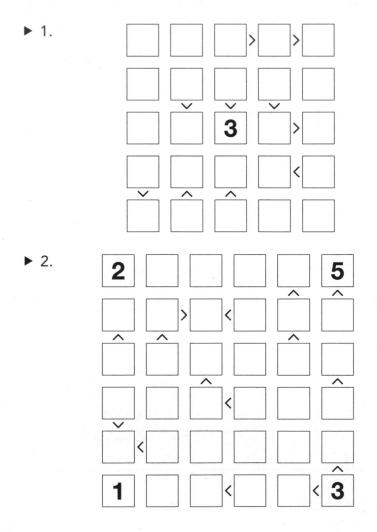

DAY 18: EXERCISE 3

Can you draw exactly three straight lines to divide each image up so that there is exactly one of each different shape in every resulting area?

▶ 1.

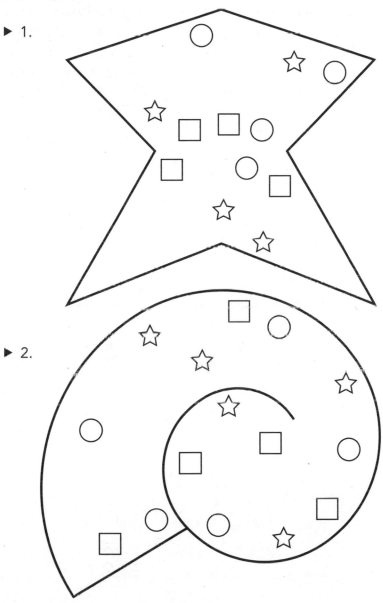

▶ 2.

DAY 19 YOUR SOCIAL BRAIN

+ Social contact is important for a healthy brain
+ It's natural to want to fit in with people around us
+ Interaction with other people can help free your mind

WHAT?

No matter who you are, social contact with other human beings is important for your brain. We have evolved to live together, and life can be much tougher without regular social contact.

WHY?

Social contact requires you to pay attention and focus. It's impossible to get through a proper conversation without listening, thinking and responding sensibly. It can also help alleviate stress, since sharing a problem can make it seem more manageable – and talking to other people often distracts you from your own thoughts. Time spent with friends or family can also at least temporarily free you from the concerns of having to make decisions on your own.

Suggested time to spend
20 MINUTES

► TRY IT ◄

DAY 19: EXERCISE 1

These logical- and lateral-thinking puzzles might be easier to solve if discussed with a friend – or a couple of friends. So you could consider setting them aside to try later, with others.

► The day before yesterday I was 8 years old. Next year I'm going to be 11 years old. How can this be?

► Which of these words is the odd one out? Triangle; Learning; Altering; Integral; Relating

► How many '5's do you need to write out all of the numbers between 1 and 100 using digits?

► I fell straight onto a concrete floor from the top of a five-metre ladder, and yet wasn't hurt at all. Why not?

► What is special about the number 8,549,176,320?

► Dominica, Kiribati and Suriname are three countries that all consist of alternative vowels and consonants. There is one country with a longer name that obeys the same rule. What is it?

► What do the following words all have in common? Sleep; Decal; Retool; Warder; Deliver; Spoons.

► Two mothers and two daughters each bought a necklace at the same time, and yet there were only three necklaces bought in total. How is that so?

► What always runs behind time?

► TRY IT ◄

DAY 19: EXERCISE 2

See if you can come up with some punchlines for these jokes, either on your own or by discussing ideas with others.

► Why did the aardvark cross the road?

_____

► What's the difference between a paper fastener and a horse stall?

_____

► What do you call a one-eyed giant?

_____

► Red, yellow and blue get together in a paint pot and have a conversation. They say:

_____

_____

► What do you get if you cross a frog and a leaf?

_____

DAY 19: EXERCISE 3

Can you work out the film titles represented by each set of initials? Each film is in IMDB.com's list of the top 50 highest-rated films of all time.

TGTBATE

BTTF

TLOTRTROTK

OFOTCN

AIW

TSOTL

SPR

LIB

SMARTER INTERACTION

+ Explaining things to others can lead to new realizations
+ Sometimes a lack of knowledge can be helpful
+ Large groups don't necessarily help so much

WHAT?

When you talk to others, you are forced to think about things in a different way. Vocalizing concepts and problems forces your brain to treat them differently, which can in and of itself help you come up with new ideas – or spot problems. Similarly, others can help trigger new thoughts even if they are not knowledgeable about a particular subject.

WHY?

Explaining something out loud uses different brain circuitry to simply thinking about it, and even an uninformed response to an explanation can sometimes trigger helpful new ideas. Also, a need to explain basic facts to others can sometimes help you spot previously unnoticed flaws in earlier assumptions.

Suggested time to spend
25 MINUTES

▶ TRY IT ◀

OTHER VOICES

Even if you are the unquestioned expert on a subject, it's often helpful to talk through your conclusions and problems with others. It can trigger new thoughts, or help highlight faulty thinking.

Larger groups, however, can have the opposite effect:

> ▶ **The larger the group, the more likely it is that one person will dominate the conversation**

> ▶ **In larger groups, there may be hierarchies which lead to a lack of balance, or silence certain voices**

> ▶ **The larger a group, the more likely it is that someone will object to an agreement**

> ▶ **With more voices, the more likely a discussion is to wander off topic**

DAY 20: EXERCISE 1

Is there a decision you have been thinking about recently, or a problem you are trying to solve? If so, write out a brief description of the problem:

_____

Now try explaining, out loud, the main points that you have considered so far, and any deductions you have made. If there's someone to talk to then that's great, but you can also simply talk to yourself. Does the process help you think more deeply?

DAY 20: EXERCISE 2

Draw either a corner, straight or crossing line segment in every square of this grid, in a similar way to those that are already given. The aim is to create a single loop that visits every square. The loop can only consist of horizontal and vertical lines.

▶ 1.

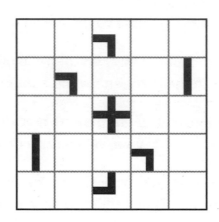

▶ 2.

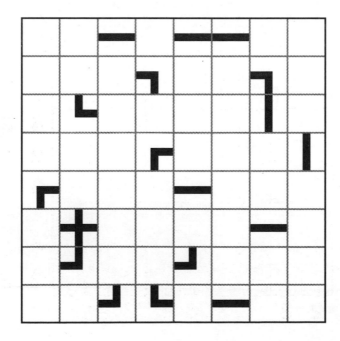

► TRY IT ◄

DAY 20: EXERCISE 3

Place a digit from 1 to 9 into each empty square, so that each digit appears exactly once in every row, column and bold-lined 3×3 box.

Numbers outside the grid must be placed into the same row or column in the nearest 3×3 box, but not necessarily in the order given.

For example, the '9 and 6' at the top must be placed in some way into the first three squares of the first column, and a '2' must be placed into one of the bottom three squares of the same column.

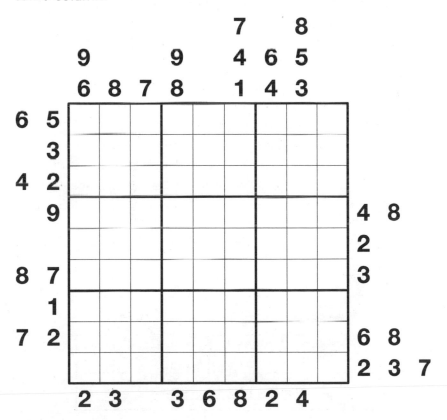

IGNORANCE OF GROUPS

+ Don't blindly assume that others know better than you
+ Groups don't always act rationally
+ It's important to think for yourself, and not be swayed

WHAT?

In large groups, we tend to behave differently. If a crowd of people are all acting in a particular way, it's natural to feel we must act in the same manner – even if that isn't sensible. Large groups can also cause us to doubt ourselves, even on things we were previously sure about.

WHY?

Few of us want to 'stand out from the crowd', so we copy widespread behaviour even if we don't understand it. If a fire alarm goes off, you might well feel compelled to stay put if you don't see anyone else move – even if it makes you nervous. Due to evolutionary instincts we naturally assume that we should act with the group, but in a modern society these instincts aren't always helpful.

Suggested time to spend
12 MINUTES

FEAR OF GROUPS

The larger a group, the more likely we are to assume that the group knows what it is doing. This also means that dealing with a group, as for example in making a presentation, can feel far more intimidating than dealing with individuals. Perhaps we fear being shown up for a mistake, but the truth is that it works both ways – most people in a group are afraid to ask difficult questions in case they in turn reveal their own ignorance. Those who do ask questions tend to be those with the least knowledge on a subject, and are therefore the easiest to respond to.

DEALING WITH GROUPS

If you find dealing with groups difficult then a small amount of preparation can help. Those listening to you will not have prepared as you have, so despite a natural tendency for many people to doubt themselves the truth is that you are likely to know more than the people you are talking to. And if you are talking about a subject you are an expert on then bear in mind that, although *you* may know what you do not know, other people will not have this knowledge.

It's also worth remembering that, paradoxically, it's easier to be certain about something when you don't know much about it. So, unless you know otherwise, then it is likely that those with the most confidence about a conclusion or belief are, in fact, those who are the least knowledgeable on a subject.

Finally, while it's always worth preparing for a presentation, you should also be careful not to *over*-prepare. If you plan every word or sentence then you place a lot of pressure on yourself not to lose your flow or forget something. It's better to just have bullet-point notes – unless you are reading from a script.

DAY 21: EXERCISE 1

Can you reveal a list of fruit by deleting one letter from each pair? For example, QP EF GA RD would become PEAR as follows: ~~Q~~P E~~F~~ ~~G~~A R~~D~~.

▶ OP RT AE NA GB ED

▶ PA PA PA LA EP

▶ RS DA SA MP SB EA GR RD YS

▶ DM AE TN GE OM

▶ PR EA AV EC KH

▶ AD OP RN UI CT SO TY

▶ PR EL UA MT

▶ BA PA NP LA UN AM

► TRY IT ◄

DAY 21: EXERCISE 2

Use your observation skills to sort this group of six pictures into three sets of two.

Each pair of images should be identical, apart from being rotated relative to one another. Each pair has a small visual difference from the other two pairs.

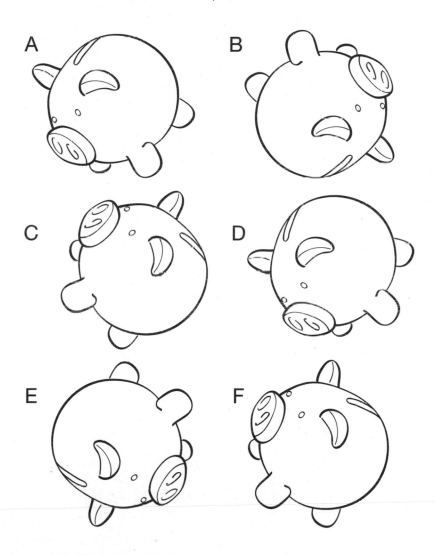

A   B

C   D

E   F

SOCIAL MEDIA

+ People often present a false impression online
+ Don't judge yourself by comparison with others
+ Not everyone writes online as they do elsewhere

WHAT?

Most of us keep track of many of our friends and family via social media, checking in to see what they have been up to, or are posting about. The upside is a sense of connectedness, but the downside is that it often appears others are living a better, more exciting life than us.

WHY?

Few of us like to share news of our failures or disappointments, so online postings are inevitably self-selected to show only one side of a person's life. What's more, they may not even be accurate representations – photos may be misleading, and jokes, opinions and more may all be copied from elsewhere. Written text also carries only limited nuance, so social media conversations can lead to misunderstandings.

Suggested time to spend
10 MINUTES

DAY 22: EXERCISE 1

Try these numeric calculations.

▶ If you have 200 friends on a social media platform, and allow your posts to be visible to friends of friends, then how many people could potentially see a single post of yours? Assume that the average number of friends that each person has is 150.

▶ If you follow 1,000 people on a social media platform, but only 50 of them follow you back, then what percentage of all the people you followed have returned the favour?

▶ If you cross-post the same image to two social media platforms, and share 50 per cent of your followers/friends across the two platforms, then what is the maximum number of distinct followers who could see the image, given that you have 100 followers on each platform? Assume that the image will be visible to all followers/friends and no one else.

DAY 22: EXERCISE 2

By adding together two or more of these numbers, can you form each of the totals below?

6 8 11 7 10 4

Totals:
20   26   30   34

DAY 22: EXERCISE 3

These six pictures can be rearranged to form a 2×3 grid that contains a letter of the alphabet. Can you work out what that letter is? Try to do this without cutting them out and physically reassembling them. Note that you'll have to rotate the pieces.

▶ TRY IT ◀

DAY 22: EXERCISE 4

Every other letter has been deleted from this list of geographical features.

Can you restore all of the missing letters to reveal the original words?

▶ _R_H_P_L_G_

▶ P_N_N_U_A

▶ _U_D_A

▶ S_V_N_A_

▶ _I_E_B_D

▶ G_A_I_R

SAYING SORRY

+ Other people won't spot your faults as easily as you do
+ If you make a mistake, apologize once and move on
+ Don't keep reminding people of things you got wrong

WHAT?

When we make a mistake, particularly one we are embarrassed about, it's tempting to apologize. And then, to make sure it's really clear we're sorry, to apologize again. And then perhaps again when we leave, or send our next email too.

WHY?

If you are late for a meeting, or make a mistake that people notice, then apologize as soon as you can. But then, having apologized, don't apologize again. If you repeat the same apology you simply make it far more memorable than it otherwise would be. Generally the first apology will show that you acknowledge your lateness/error, and that's that. People will usually forget about it – unless you keep reminding them by apologizing again!

Suggested time to spend
15 MINUTES

▶ IN DEPTH ◀

POINTING OUT ERRORS

We are more conscious of our own failings than others are. Most people are so wrapped up in their own worlds that they don't notice the mistakes others make. Sometimes they have made their own mistakes, and are hoping *you* don't notice them. So don't go out of your way to point out your faults – let others spot them, and then by all means apologize if appropriate. Of course, in some situations it's important to point out errors, but generally in life there is no benefit to putting yourself down.

OVER-APOLOGIZING

It's worth thinking through what happens if you apologize too many times – and just once is usually enough.

Pretend that you are late for a meeting, and you apologize. Unless you were so unspeakably late that it's all they can think about, the chances are the other person will essentially forget about your lateness after a short while. You then leave the meeting and apologize once again for having been late, thinking you are being polite. But in fact they have forgotten you were late, since that happened some while back, and all you have done is remind them of it. Now they leave the meeting remembering that you were late. The moral of the story is simple: by all means apologize, but then don't remind people again. It isn't necessary, and there is *no* benefit to you.

On a related note, when you *do* apologize then don't overdo it. Say that you're sorry and move on. There's generally no need to make a big fuss about it, and say how it will never happen again or some such melodramatic statement. All this will do is draw extra attention, and make it far more memorable.

DAY 23: EXERCISE 1

Can you form each of the given totals by choosing one number from each ring of this number dart board?

For example, you could form a total of 49 by picking 15 from the innermost ring, 22 from the central ring and 12 from the outermost ring.

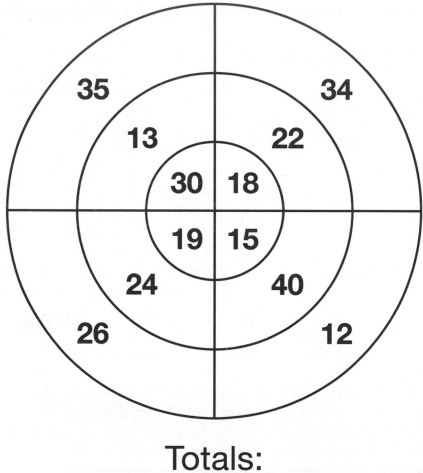

Totals:
58   70   80

DAY 23: EXERCISE 2

Solve these number anagrams by rearranging the given numbers and mathematical operators until they result in the target number shown. You must use all of the numbers and operators when reaching the result.

You can use any number of parentheses (brackets) to arrange the numbers when writing out your calculation. For example, 3 4 5 + × could be arranged to make 35 like this: (3+4)×5=35.

► 1.   Target = 19

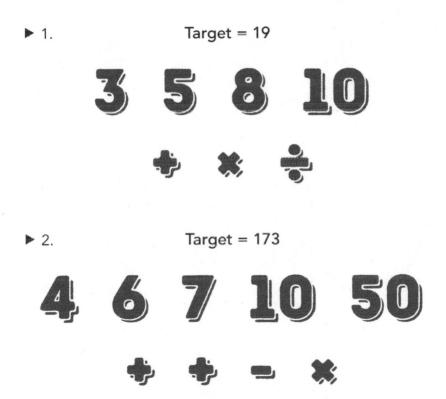

► 2.   Target = 173

DAY 24 COLLECTIVE MEMORY

+ People remember successes much more than failures
+ Those who take risks tend to look brave
+ Whereas those who are careful and prudent look weak

WHAT?

It's an unfortunate characteristic of human behaviour that reckless behaviour often appears to be brave and daring, rather than simply reckless and stupid as it probably really is. Conversely, careful and considerate decisions can seem cowardly rather than sensible.

WHY?

You can probably think of several prominent politicians who appear to lack both shame and competence, and yet they are in power. How? They have relied – whether knowingly or not – on the self-selecting power of people to focus on the characteristics and results they most prefer. We often choose to believe that the parts of somebody's character we like are in fact the 'real them'.

Suggested time to spend
12 MINUTES

BEING BRAVE

Those who have most success in business are often those who take the most risks – even reckless ones. We tend to remember a person's successes rather than their failures, and so when someone cherry picks their victories from a life also full of failures then they tend to be hailed as a visionary. No matter that they may have lost investors' money on several occasions, they are seen as someone who has the potential to bring further success.

While it isn't usually sensible to be reckless, sometimes in life it's necessary to act at least a bit as others may do. Don't draw attention to the problems with a plan you're proposing, or point out what has gone wrong in the past. Other people may not point out the flaws in their competing proposals, and so you will lose out as a result of human psychology. If you want to gain advancement in a job, focus on your achievements and say what you want to do next; don't dwell on the present, or be afraid to suggest significant change.

EASY FIXES

It's tempting to believe that there are easy fixes in life, and human psychology tempts us towards those who claim to offer them. For example, if you've ever believed that you can 'detox' your body by drinking or eating certain specific foods then you've been misled. Whole industries exist to sell health and beauty products with scientific-sounding claims that in reality are not actually backed by science. They sound good, and the desire to believe in them is so strong that people will praise them for their perceived benefits – even if the benefits aren't real. We focus on the things we agree with and choose to believe in, excluding alternative opinions as wrong or malign.

► TRY IT ◄

DAY 24: EXERCISE 1

Which connects all of the items in each of these sets?

► Sun, Trident, Star, Maple leaf

► Uniform, Hotel, November, Echo

► Leading, Stroke, Tracking, Baseline

► Bounce, Small, Jelly, Noisy

► Beam, Floor, Vault, Bars

► Capital, Security, Trust, Future

► Coral, North, Red, Ross

► Dover, Olympia, Jackson, Lincoln

► Monroe, Arthur, Jackson, Lincoln

► TRY IT ◄

DAY 24: EXERCISE 2

Can you complete each of these number pyramids by writing a value into every empty brick? Each brick should contain a value equal to the sum of the two bricks immediately beneath it. (The bottom row can contain any values, so along as the rules are followed for the rest of the pyramid.)

 1.

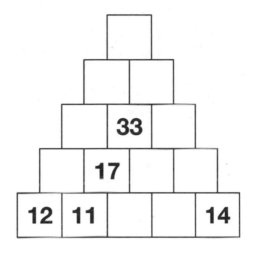

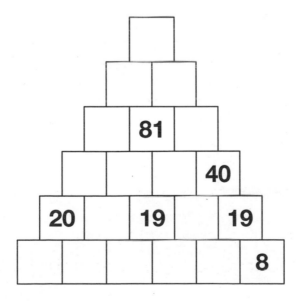 2.

DAY 25 RELATIONS WITH OTHERS

+ We don't always say what we intend, or hear accurately
+ It's easy to talk at cross-purposes with other people
+ It's not sensible to rely on other people changing

WHAT?

Relationships with others, especially close relationships, can be challenging. Everyone is different, yet we have a tendency to project our own assumptions onto other people. Not everyone thinks the same way we do, or has the same experience as us.

WHY?

It's said that familiarity breeds contempt, and the more time you spend with someone the less tolerant you are likely to become of them. It's human nature to slowly get more and more irritated by something that initially is only a minor annoyance, and yet it's unrealistic to expect other people to change in a significant way. This can lead relationships to have built-in expiry dates, where eventually the sum of all accumulated annoyances, grievances and disagreements outweighs the positives.

Suggested time to spend
20 MINUTES

► IN DETAIL ◄

FOCUSING ON FAILINGS

Yesterday we looked at how collectively we remember successes and forget failures. In relationships, however, the opposite effect can often take hold. We focus on problems and failings, and forget about all the good times we've spent with others.

There can, of course, be serious problems in relationships, and these must be dealt with – quite possibly by avoiding all further contact. But, for day-to-day disagreements, much of what causes people to fall out is due ultimately to misunderstandings. Perhaps a careless, unthinking decision is thought to be deliberate, rather than simply thoughtless, making it harder to repair. Or, in a conversation, two people may have different intentions without realizing, leading to fundamental disagreements about what was said and where each is convinced that the other is solely at fault.

All this said, if a relationship is seriously one-sided then it isn't a good one. Having a sense of balance is very different to accepting behaviour which is domineering or exploitative. People are unlikely to significantly change their personalities, so don't wait around for a change that will never come.

MISCOMMUNICATION

Sometimes we mishear words, or conversely people mishear us. But, in relationships, miscommunications can go deeper. Some people like to give or receive gifts as a token of friendship, which may not have the same significance to the other person. Other areas where people's expectations can differ without them realizing include how much time they spend together, how much they help one another, how much praise they give or receive, and issues to do with physical contact.

DAY 25: EXERCISE 1

Place an arrow into each of the dashed-line boxes, so that each arrow points either up, down, left, right or in one of the four main diagonal directions.

For each puzzle, you must place the arrows so that each number is pointed at by that many arrows.

▶ 1.

2	4	2
6	2	5
2	3	0

▶ 2.

2	3	8	4
1	3	4	5
3	1	4	3
2	2	3	2

DAY 25: EXERCISE 2

Draw a loop which passes through some of the empty squares. The loop can only travel horizontally and vertically between squares, and it cannot enter a square more than once. It therefore also can't cross over itself.

Draw the loop in such a way that each number reveals how many touching squares the loop passes through, including diagonally touching squares.

▶ 1.

3			5		
	7		7		
3			3		

▶ 2.

	3		4				2
						3	
4		6					2
			7				
					7		
	7						
						3	

DAY 26

TAKE A GUESS

+ Children learn by experimentation – and so can adults
+ Fear of failure may hold us back from trying things out
+ You never know what you can do until you try

WHAT?

When you were a baby, you learned to walk by physically experimenting, without fear of falling over. Then, gradually as you got older, you may have become less and less keen to try something completely new, perhaps for fear of failure. By the time we reach old age, many of us are set in our ways and think that we can't learn anything significantly new anymore.

WHY?

It's easy to sit back and relax into a life of a fixed set of activities, where you are secure in the knowledge that you know what you are doing. But the truth is that your brain can learn really quickly, spotting patterns and making deductions. It adapts to new situations incredibly quickly, and what at first seems overwhelmingly hard may soon seem entirely manageable.

Suggested time to spend
25 MINUTES

▶ IN DEPTH ◀

A FIRST STEP

Guessing is a good strategy for 'getting going' on a project or problem. It might sound strange, but if you don't know what to do then it's better to just start somewhere than sit around without making any progress. So long as you aren't going to cause any irrevocable damage, it doesn't really matter how you begin.

Just the very act of starting can help you overcome the problem of inertia. What's more, even if your initial guess (or proposal) turns out to be off the mark then you will still learn something in the process. Understanding *why* it won't work gives you insights into the underlying task or problem. In most cases you'll learn a lot faster by trying and failing, than by sitting and studying.

GET GOING WITH PUZZLES

You can use this technique with the puzzles in this book. Some of them might seem intimidatingly complex to solve, but the truth is that if you put in an initial guess then you'll soon start to get to grips with it. Understanding if that guess fits with the rules of the puzzle helps make the instructions concrete, and working out why it does – or doesn't – helps you make progress to the solution and lets your brain start to learn the ins and outs of the puzzle's logic.

Not all guesses will necessarily be particularly helpful, but if your first guess doesn't benefit you then make a second one. And a third. Keep experimenting, and if you reach an impasse then take a good look at the puzzle and see what isn't working with your solution. Perhaps there is only a small adjustment needed somewhere that will make it all work out.

▶ TRY IT ◀

DAY 26: EXERCISE 1

A maze is the classic guessing puzzle, so it makes sense to start by trying this circular maze.

The aim is simple: find your way through, entering at the top and exiting at the bottom.

DAY 26: EXERCISE 2

Draw a series of separate paths, each connecting a pair of identical numbers or letters. No more than one line can enter any square, and lines can only travel horizontally or vertically between the centres of squares.

▶ 1.

▶ 2.

DAY 26: EXERCISE 3

Find a hidden snake in the grid by obeying the clues:

▶ Numbers at the start of some rows and columns reveal the number of squares occupied by the snake in that row/column.

▶ The snake is a continuous path of shaded squares that does not touch itself at any point, not even diagonally (except by virtue of turning a corner). See the example to the right to see how this works.

▶ The start and end of the snake are given.

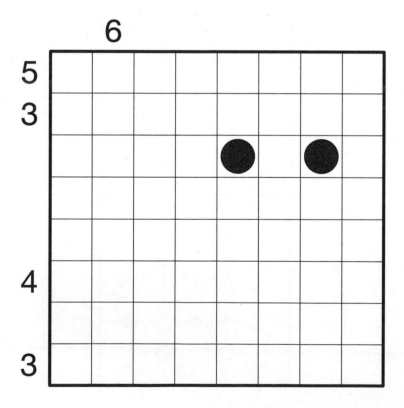

▶ TRY IT ◀

DAY 26: EXERCISE 4

Place the digits 1 to 9 once each into each 3×3 grid so that:

▶ Numbers separated by a white dot are consecutive, such as 2 and 3, or 7 and 8.
▶ Numbers separated by a black dot have one double the value of the other, such as 2 and 4, or 3 and 6.
▶ Numbers *not* separated by a dot must be neither consecutive nor have one be double the other.
▶ 1 and 2, if touching, may be separated by either a black dot or a white dot.

▶ 1.

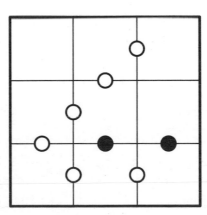

▶ 2.

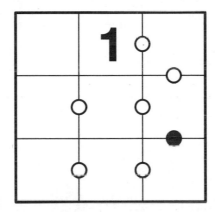

DAY 27 AUTOMATIC RESPONSES

+ Your brain is constructed in layers, going back in time
+ Your conscious brain doesn't have full control
+ Many of the core bodily processes are automated

WHAT?

You don't have full control over your body. You can hold your breath for a bit, but you can't will yourself to stop breathing. You might know that you have had enough to eat, but you can't tell your body to ignore hunger pangs. You also can't acknowledge that something is hurting and switch off the pain.

WHY?

Your brain consists of evolutionary recent structures on top of much older, more primitive parts. They coordinate the movement of your muscles, allowing you to think 'I want to move my hand there' rather than worry about each individual muscle movement. And they deal with critical signals such as hunger, thirst, pain and more.

Suggested time to spend
10 MINUTES

OVERRULING YOURSELF

Certain behaviours which you share with other animals, such as freezing in situations of sudden extreme danger or confusion, can be very unhelpful in our modern lives. If you're caught in the middle of a road as a car speeds towards you, freezing is not likely to be the best response. And, as we've already seen, your herd instinct to copy other people can cause you to make foolish decisions that go against your own instincts.

FALSE URGENCY

Sometimes our brains mislead us. We think we had better eat something while we can, even though we know that we could still eat it later – or eat something else, even. Primitive responses that were designed to help get you through lean times are not of benefit to us when we have easy access to ready supplies of food.

A similar behaviour is exploited by store sales. They create a false sense of urgency – that you had better buy something now while it is cheaper, or before it sells out – to rush you into decisions that you might not have made had you taken the time to think about them more dispassionately.

QUESTION YOUR JUDGEMENT

As you get older, you gain experience which – in general – allows you to make more sensible decisions than you might once have done. As part of this, it is worth taking time to think about decisions you now think were wrong. If they were based on gut feelings, how might your instincts have let you down? You can then look out for similarly misleading conclusions in future.

DAY 27: EXERCISE 1

Try these optical illusions, to see if you can spot the automatic responses in your visual system! First up, which of the five lines on the right represents the continuation of the straight line shown on the left?

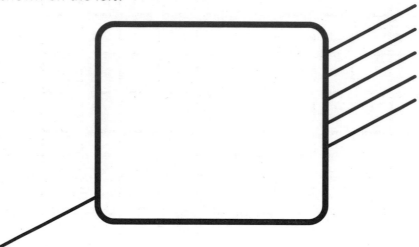

DAY 27: EXERCISE 2

Are these two horizontal lines straight, or do they bend?

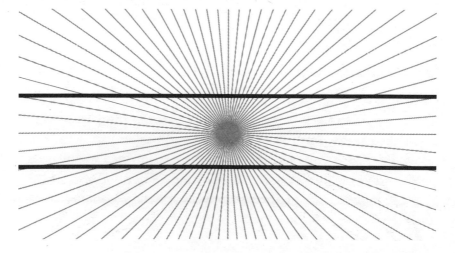

DAY 27: EXERCISE 3

Do you see a grid of straight lines with some gaps, or do you see a grid that is covered by an array of white circles?

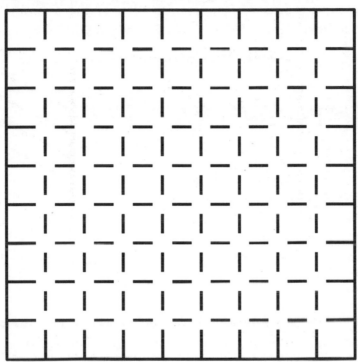

DAY 27: EXERCISE 4

Here are parts of three different circles. If you could see the rest of each circle, would they all be different sizes or would they all be the same size?

DAY 28 CONSCIOUS THOUGHT

+ You aren't consciously aware of all of your thoughts
+ Your brain can carry on thinking while you sleep
+ Expressing things in different forms helps unlock ideas

WHAT?

You are only consciously aware of a tiny part of what goes on in your brain. Where, after all, do the words you speak come from? Do they just appear as if by magic in your mind and mouth? And how is it you can brush your teeth while reading?

WHY?

Do you ever find yourself unexpectedly coming up with ideas, or solutions to problems you thought about a while ago? If so, you have your unconscious mind to thank. You are only capable of consciously thinking about one thing at a time, but this doesn't stop the rest of your brain from carrying on working. In particular, while you sleep your brain is ferociously busy, making sense of the day that has gone and thinking up new solutions to problems you have.

Suggested time to spend
15 MINUTES

AUTOMATIC BEHAVIOURS

Physical processes that you perform over and over start to become at least semi automated. This is how you can learn to walk, ride a bicycle or drive a car. When you start to drive you have to concentrate on every movement of your hands and feet, but it soon becomes second nature – to the point where you can perhaps follow a common route and suddenly realize you are doing so on what amounts to auto-pilot!

These learned physical skills are critical to us being able to live life, but it's the even higher level abilities of your brain to carry on working without you that are truly astonishing. Some scientists describe your brain as having loops of thought that carry on within it without you being consciously aware of them.

SLEEP

Sleep might be a time of rest for your conscious mind, but your unconscious mind is as busy as ever while you sleep. It runs over the day you've just had, filing away memories and making sense of everything you experienced. Sleep plays such an important role in storing memory that when you are trying to memorize material you should take particular care to ensure you do not disturb your sleep too much.

In the hours after you wake you might find yourself coming up – seemingly spontaneously – with new ideas or conclusions that your brain came up with while you were fast asleep. If anyone has ever told you to 'sleep on it' they were not only telling you to take your time, but also giving you invaluable advice on how best to take advantage of the power of your brain!

▶ TRY IT ◀

DAY 28: EXERCISE 1

Try these puzzles. If you get stuck, why not leave them overnight – or for a few hours – and see if you can make progress when you return to them?

How many recent former summer Olympic host countries can you list? See if you can fill them in by year:

▶ 1992: _____

▶ 1996: _____

▶ 2000: _____

▶ 2004: _____

▶ 2008: _____

▶ 2012: _____

▶ 2016: _____

▶ TRY IT ◀

DAY 28: EXERCISE 2

Now see how many recent US presidents you can list. The years they were in office are shown at the start of each line.

▶ 1969–74:_____

▶ 1974–77:_____

▶ 1977–81:_____

▶ 1981–89:_____

▶ 1989–93:_____

▶ 1993–2001:_____

▶ 2001–09:_____

▶ 2009–17:_____

SEEMINGLY MEANINGFUL

+ Coincidences are surprisingly common
+ Your brain likes to spot patterns even where none exist
+ Try to avoid jumping to false conclusions

WHAT?

Your brain is a phenomenal pattern-spotting machine. It spots and notices things that appear to happen together or in sequence, giving you a chance to work out what's going on and learn about the world. Unfortunately, it also spots patterns where none exist.

WHY?

Spotting patterns lets your brain give you quick, accurate information. Rapidly recognizing a person's face, or noticing that lightning comes shortly after thunder, are useful. But your brain is also capable of spotting patterns where none exist, such as in coin tosses or in coincidental occurrences.

Suggested time to spend
12 MINUTES

▶ IN DEPTH ◀

DISCOUNTING COINCIDENCE

You think of a friend, and then all of a sudden they get in touch. Or you talk about a place, and then hear it mentioned on the radio later that day. Or perhaps you get chatting to someone in a shop who turns out to have the same birthday as you.

These coincidences seem very impressive, and so your brain attaches importance to them – they must have some meaning. But the truth is that you are simply *noticing* the coincidence. Most of the time, when you think of a friend, they don't immediately call you – so why, on the occasions when this does happen, do you attach any more importance to it than any other time they call? A similar explanation applies to most coincidences.

SUCCESS EXTRAPOLATION

If you try something risky and you succeed, it's tempting to believe that you'll be successful if you try it again. Your brain almost immediately starts to overestimate your skill, leading to a false sense of certainty. Surprisingly, these false feelings of safety will tend to remain even after failure. Successes are attributed to skill, while failures are attributed to bad luck.

There are various biases in human psychology that tend towards an optimistic view of the world, and this is one of them. Perhaps without this it would have been hard for us to spread around the globe – much safer to stay put, rather than try anything new. There is indeed nothing wrong with a positive bias – and in fact it's generally desirable, so long as it isn't taken to excess. And if you are aware of it then you can take it into consideration when making decisions, wherever relevant.

▶ TRY IT ◀

DAY 29: EXERCISE 1

Have you ever come across strange acronyms, such as TLDR, WYSIWYG or others and not been sure what they stand for? Well, now it's time to make up your *own* acronyms!

What do you think each of the following acronyms could stand for? There are no correct answers here.

▶ EUDG

▶ TASA

▶ WHOOP

▶ NONO

▶ ROBOTT

▶ TEAPOT

▶ SLUDGE

▶ TRY IT ◀

DAY 29: EXERCISE 2

Each of the following sentences contains a hidden sport. See if you can find them all.

▶ I put the bad mint on the table – I did not like it!

▶ The Delphi king sat upon his throne

▶ I always think about the dress age when getting ready to go out

▶ The guy from Dakar ate only fish and chips

▶ This nook erases all hint of light

▶ The retro deodorant smelled strange

▶ He took the drug by oral application

DAY
30 THE UNEXPECTED

+ It can be hard to cope when the unexpected happens
+ But making plans for future events prepares your brain
+ In a crisis, it's important to stay focused

WHAT?

From time to time, things happen that are outside our experience or expectations. If these put us in danger, or threaten us in some way, then we often don't react very rationally. Our fears can overtake us, leading us to a helplessness whereby we don't move to get out of danger, whether literally or metaphorically.

WHY?

Your brain comes with built-in behaviours to deal with danger. Your blood is flooded with adrenaline, and your heart rate increases. Your perception of time may change, so events appear to run more slowly. Primitive animal behaviours may also kick in, so you lose access to your higher-level human skills.

Suggested time to spend
20 MINUTES

▶ IN DEPTH ◀

PREPARING RESPONSES

You can't spend your life worrying about what might happen, but spend a few minutes thinking about what you would do if there were a fire in your house, or if you were locked out without keys. Do you know exactly what you would do in those situations? If not, think them through so you can act sensibly if they ever did – or in the case of keys, prepare a back-up in advance.

Although it might sound morbid, it's worth thinking through what you would do in various different serious situations. In this way, should such an event ever occur, you will be better able to respond more sensibly because your conscious mind will be prepared.

In traumatic real-life events, people sometimes appear to be paralysed and unable to move. They are frozen in their place by shock, since the stimuli arriving at their brain are too overwhelming to process. To help pre-empt this, think through what you would do if you were ever caught up in such an event. Make sure your brain has done some initial thinking, so in a real-life situation it has more chance of responding sensibly. These don't need to be complex preparations, but simply thinking about what your initial reactions could be – such as running away.

UNEXPECTED OTHERS

Other people do unexpected things too – including things that don't make sense, even to them. It's therefore also wise to have thought through how you might deal with other people in a case of emergency. In extreme situations people do not act rationally and they can endanger you with their behaviour.

▶ TRY IT ◀

DAY 30: EXERCISE 1

Think of some situations it might make sense to prepare for:

▶ 1: _____

▶ 2: _____

▶ 3: _____

Now make a simple plan for each of the above:

▶ 1: _____

_____

▶ 2: _____

_____

▶ 3: _____

_____

DAY 30: EXERCISE 2

Complete this confusing sudoku puzzle by placing a number from 1 to 9 into every empty white square. You must place numbers so that no number appears more than once in any row, column or bold-lined 3×3 box.

Unexpectedly, the shaded squares (which you do not write a number in) can 'represent' a different missing digit in each of the row, column and box they are in.

1			7	4	6		▓	3
		2	3	▓		8		
	3	▓			9	4	1	
2		3	▓		1		7	6
9	1						2	▓
6	▓		8		2	5		1
	8	1	6			▓	9	
▓		9		2	4	1		
3			1	9	▓			4

EXPECTATION BIAS

+ **We make biased decisions all the time**
+ **We are more likely to believe things we want to be true**
+ **Your brain uses simple rules that may mislead you**

WHAT?

Most people believe they are capable of making fair, unbiased decisions. But in reality our brains nudge us along in the direction of believing things we already hope or suspect to be true. We also sometimes 'feel' that things must be true based on simple rules that our brains use – and which can be wrong.

WHY?

We often need to make quick decisions, and so our brains have evolved to allow us to do just that, suggesting snap judgements on almost everything. These instinctive feelings that guide our thought processes can be helpful, but if we aren't aware that they happen then they can also sometimes seriously mislead us.

Suggested time to spend
20 MINUTES

TYPES OF BIAS

We have many types of mental bias, all of which can affect our expectations. Some include:

► We assume that groups are more likely to be correct than individuals

► We make poor estimates of probabilities

► We still assume that future events are influenced by past ones, even when it is clear that they cannot be connected

► We believe that specific occurrences that match our expectations are more likely to occur than less specific ones

► We ignore information which contradicts our beliefs

► We think we could have predicted past events, even when we didn't actually do so

► The more we hear something, the more it seems likely to be true to us

► We happily scale up from a tiny amount of information to general conclusions

► We readily ignore information which contradicts our beliefs

► We apply stereotypes about groups to individuals

DEALING WITH BIAS

It can be incredibly difficult to deal with bias, because we don't even realize we are *being* biased. The best we can do is try to avoid making snap decisions in areas in which we know that our brains take unfortunate shortcuts.

One area where our estimations are particularly unhelpful is when dealing with probabilities – as many a gambler discovers.

COINCIDENTAL NUMBERS

If there are 23 people in a room, the chances are *more likely than not* that two of them share the same birthday. It may sound unlikely, but that's only because your brain unhelpfully imagines the chance of just *you* sharing a birthday with someone, which is much lower. In this imaginary room, there are 23 people who might share a date with 22 others, giving over 250 possible pairings to consider. Given this number, it now seems much more credible that one of those 250 pairs might share a birthday. But our initial expectations are completely wrong.

DISCONNECTED EVENTS

We also link together events that seem to be related to us in some way, even when rationally we know that they really are not. For example, if you were to toss a coin several times then, in advance of doing so, you would expect a roughly even number of heads and tails. But, from this sensible expectation, we then incorrectly conclude that what has happened in the past can influence the future. If we have just seen five heads come up, we feel we are more likely than not to have a tail next. But the truth is that the chances of either heads or tails for the next coin remain exactly equal, no matter what has gone before.

▶ TRY IT ◀

DAY 31: EXERCISE 1

Take a look at the arrangement of shapes below. How many rectangles, of all different sizes, can you count in this picture? There are more than you might think – including, for example, the large one that forms the border of the picture.

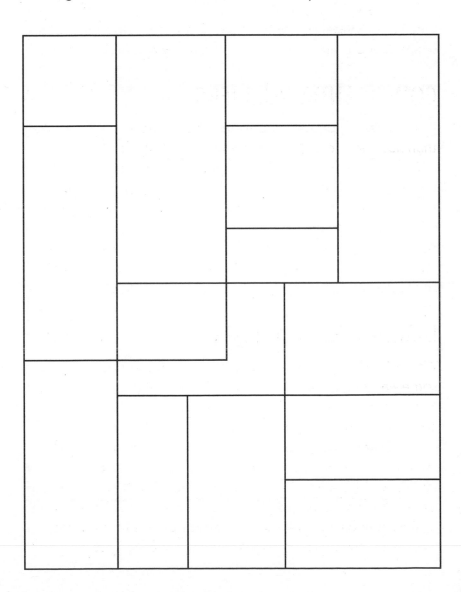

DAY 31: EXERCISE 2

Place a number from 1 to 8 into each empty square, so that no letter repeats in any row or column.

Some intersections between sets of four squares have four small digits written on them. These four digits must be placed into the four touching squares, although not necessarily in the order given.

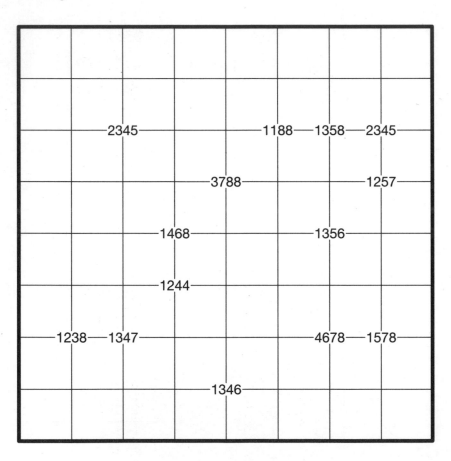

► TRY IT ◄

DAY 31: EXERCISE 3

Imagine that you start with the 5×4×4 arrangement of cubes as shown here, and then remove some. Given that none of the cubes are floating in mid-air, how many cubes remain in each of the pictures below?

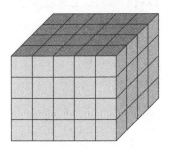

► 1.

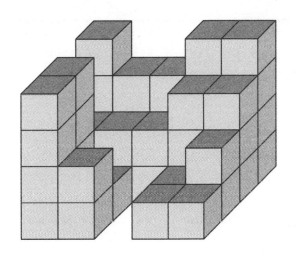

► 2.

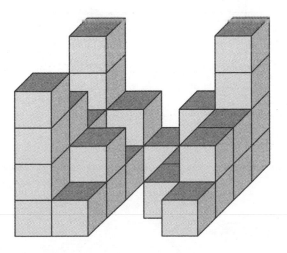

+ Be able to check your bills, and spot the *real* bargains
+ Real-world maths is nothing like school
+ Take advantage of your innate number skills

WHAT?

If 'maths' makes you think of algebra, long division and school tests, then you're missing out. Although maths in education is mostly concerned with numerical certainties, day-to-day maths is often far more relaxed. Even the least mathematically minded person can learn to make sensible numerical guesses that will help improve their life.

WHY?

Numbers are all around us, but in many Western cultures it's strangely acceptable to profess an inability to handle them. The truth is you have built-in number-reckoning skills that you can draw on. You can use those skills to avoid getting ripped off when paying the bill at a restaurant, or to have a better idea as to whether that sale item really *is* a bargain.

Suggested time to spend
10 MINUTES

DAY 32: EXERCISE 1

Take a look at these shapes. Which shape do you think there is most of? And which is there the least of? Don't count them one by one, but rather use your gut instinct to decide.

Done? There's a discussion of this puzzle on the next page, so make a note of your answers until then.

DAY 32: EXERCISE 2

Now let's try an exercise that involves actual numbers. Take a look at the figures below, and have a guess as to what you think their total value is. Just take a quick look – don't overthink it.

22 17 21 19

Now round your answer to the nearest 10, e.g. 60, 70, 80, etc.

► TRY IT ◄

QUESTIONS OF ESTIMATION

What was your answer to exercise 2? Adding up all four numbers might feel challenging, but did you estimate that the total was 80? With a little practice you can see that each number is roughly 20, and multiplying 20 by 4 is a considerably simpler proposition.

Looking back to exercise 1, the solution is that there are most squares and least triangles. Specifically, there are 9 squares, 5 triangles and 7 circles. Depending on how awake you're feeling, you might well have been able to tell at a glance which shapes there were most and least of – without actually needing to count one by one. We can often make sensible rough counting estimates, and it also gets easier with a little bit of practice.

So numbers need not necessarily involve lots of careful thought. Using sensible estimates is often all that is needed in real life. When we get to a shop checkout, or ask for the bill in a restaurant, it's good to be able to have an idea if the total is at least roughly correct.

DAY 32: EXERCISE 3

Now try estimating the result of multiplying together these eight numbers:

1 2 3 4 5 6 7 8

Have you got your total? Now estimate the result of multiplying together the eight numbers at the top of the next page.

8 7 6 5 4 3 2 1

Do you have your two guesses?

Even though the eight numbers that you are multiplying are the same in each case, it's very tempting to guess a higher result for the second sequence than the first. This is because we are biased by the numbers we see at the start of the line. In the first sequence, the first few numbers are all small so we estimate a relatively small number. But when we look at the sequence the other way round, it starts off with higher numbers so we tend to predict a higher result.

What's remarkable is that despite the fact that the two results *must* be the same, we may still somehow 'feel' that the result of the first calculation should be lower than the second. *That's* how powerful your cognitive biases can be!

DAY 32: EXERCISE 4

No catches now, but a simple maths exercise to try.

Estimate the result of adding this set of six numbers:

32 48 88
75 32 95

DAY
33 MENTAL ARITHMETIC

+ Keeping calculations in your memory can be tricky
+ Mental arithmetic can take practice to get used to
+ But working out numbers in your head is a useful skill

WHAT?

Not all calculations can be easily estimated, so practising mental arithmetic is useful for situations in which it isn't appropriate to use a calculator. Many people do so little mental arithmetic, however, that they struggle with anything more complex than adding a couple of numbers together.

WHY?

If you do more than a single calculation in your head, mental arithmetic involves remembering the result of one calculation to apply to the next calculation, and possibly similarly on in a chain of calculations. Because we rarely practise using our memory in such a way, these calculations can initially seem disproportionately challenging.

Suggested time to spend
25 MINUTES

A HEAD FOR FIGURES

Some people are capable of impressive feats of mental arithmetic, but that's not what we're talking about here. We're simply referring to the ability to perform a series of calculations without losing track of the intermediate values.

Mental arithmetic requires you to make good use of your short-term memory, which can only store a few items for less than 30 seconds. Since we are so used to writing things down, or using a calculator, we don't practise this skill much and so when we try to do so we find it much harder than we otherwise would.

Luckily, just a little practice can have a big effect, so you could try the following exercises a few times over a few days and see if you start to find them easier.

DAY 33: EXERCISE 1

Look at these three numbers, then when you think you will remember them cover them over and read the following text:

13   19   22

Now, keeping the numbers above covered, which one of the following four numbers could you form by adding together exactly two of the numbers you just memorized?

31   35   38   43

DAY 33: EXERCISE 2

How did you do with the exercise on the previous page? It can seem really tough when you first try, but it gets easier with practice.

Try each of the following sets of numbers, one at a time. After memorizing them, cover them over and see which of the corresponding totals on the opposite page you could form. Try not to look ahead at the totals.

► 1.

7   9   6

► 2.

11   13   18

► 3.

6   17   21

► 4.

31   42   50

DAY 33: EXERCISE 2 (continued)

The numbers below are for use with the same row of numbers at the same position on the directly opposite page.

If you avoid writing in the book for this exercise, you could repeat it on future days and see if you find it easier.

▶ 1.

15   18   21

▶ 2.

25   29   33

▶ 3.

22   38   32

▶ 4.

74   83   92

► TRY IT ◄

DAY 33: EXERCISE 3

See if you can solve each of these brain chains without making any written notes – i.e. using your mental arithmetic.

Start with the value on the left of each chain, then apply the operations in the order shown by the arrows until you reach the end of the chain. What is the result?

► 1.

| 29 | +9 | +50% | ÷3 | +63 | –20 | RESULT |

► 2.

| 14 | –50% | +18 | ÷5 | ×2 | –70% | RESULT |

► 3.

| 29 | ×3 | ×2/3 | +18 | ×1/2 | –50% | RESULT |

► 4.

| 27 | ×1/3 | √ | ×7 | –11 | ×1/2 | RESULT |

► 5.

| 45 | –35 | –30% | +36 | –4 | +56 | RESULT |

▶ TRY IT ◀

DAY 33: EXERCISE 4

Solve each of these calcudoku puzzles by placing 1 to 6 once each into every row and column. Also, each of the bold-lined regions must result in the given value when the operation shown is applied between all of the numbers in that region. For example, a '3+' region must add up to 3. For subtraction and division, start with the highest value in a region and subtract or divide by the rest.

▶ 1.

12×		16+			3+
11+		12×	5+		
3+				11+	
24×		1–	5+	5+	
3–	36×			8+	
				5+	

▶ 2.

9+		6×		8×	30×
1÷		4–	96×		
432×			4–	8+	
2÷	20×			54×	
		2–			

BUYER'S REMORSE

+ Shops and salespeople create a false sense of urgency
+ Sales and other time-limited discounts can mislead
+ Sellers use 'fear of missing out' to drive sales

WHAT?

You're out and about, without any intention of buying, when you come across an amazing bargain – so you buy. But have you really made a saving, or have you been misled?

WHY?

Sales, limited stock, temporary promotions, free extras and a whole host of other 'deals' are all designed to encourage you to buy. They work because we can't help but be concerned we are about to miss out on a great opportunity. But the truth is that in almost all cases the fear of missing out is illusory, created purely to play on the way that your brain works.

Suggested time to spend
25 MINUTES

SALES TECHNIQUES

In some countries, including the UK, items can only be marked as on sale if they have genuinely been sold at higher prices previously – which is why you will find Christmas products on sale in department stores from late summer, even if tucked away in a corner of a store. Then, when Christmas comes, magically everything is on sale! Or have you been to a furniture store and found that half of the items are in a temporary 50% off sale? Check back a month later and you might find that the other half of their stock is discounted instead. The 'sticker price' is a lie, intended for no purpose other than to encourage you to buy now, not later – but if you end up buying a non-discounted item at double its value, then great!

Proven sales techniques include:

▶ Free samples – especially face-to-face we often feel compelled to buy the product after trying

▶ Free gifts – even if we don't want them, we think they add extra value (and they make returns trickier)

▶ Free trials – we might not cancel or return

▶ Countdowns – time-limited or item-limited sales give a false sense of urgency

▶ Popularity – the presence of many others, or if online then people counters indicating that others are buying or about to buy a product ('15 bought this in the past hour', or '23 people are looking at this right now')

DAY 34: EXERCISE 1

Join circled numbers (islands) with horizontal or vertical lines (bridges), so that all islands are joined into a single connected network by following one or more bridges. Bridges cannot cross either each other or an island, and there can't be more than two bridges between a pair of islands. The number on each island indicates how many bridges connect to that island.

▶ 1.

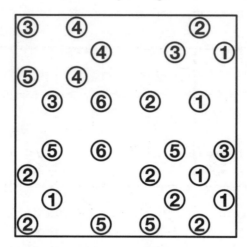

▶ 2.

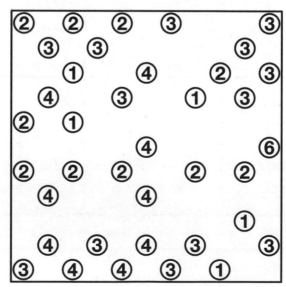

DAY 34: EXERCISE 2

Test your number skills by completing this unusual sudoku puzzle.

Place 1 to 9 once each into every row, column and bold-lined 3×3 box. Also, the number in each circled square must be equal to the total of the numbers in the squares that the attached arrow passes through.

BUILDING VOCABULARY

+ Read as widely as you can – even if just online articles
+ A wider vocabulary facilitates easier thinking
+ Consider learning a foreign language

WHAT?

Being able to express yourself clearly and concisely increases the likelihood that others will pay attention to you, and also helps you to think with greater ease. Building a good vocabulary also increases the pleasure of reading, and also helps expose your brain to new concepts and ideas.

WHY?

Being able to use fewer words to explain a concept makes it easier to hold it in both your own and others' working memories, increasing the chance that others can understand it – and making it easier to think about in the first place. Expanding your vocabulary, and your horizons in general by reading widely, helps enrich both your thought and your communication skills. Foreign languages can help too, bringing in new concepts.

Suggested time to spend
15 MINUTES

DAY 35: EXERCISE 1

The following puzzles will challenge your vocabulary.

How many words can you make in each of the following word puzzles? Start on any square and trace a path left/right/up/down from letter to letter, spelling out a word. You cannot visit a square more than once within that word. There is one word that uses every letter.

► 1.

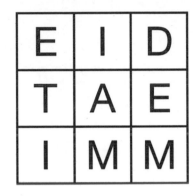

Target: 15 words

► 2.

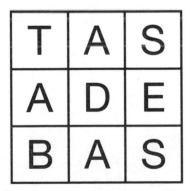

Target: 12 words

▶ TRY IT ◀

DAY 35: EXERCISE 2

All of the vowels have been deleted from the following words, and then random spaces have been inserted.

Can you restore all of the words, each of which is a shade of purple (such as 'VIOLET', for example).

▶ M GN T

▶ L VN DR

▶ N DG

▶ P LM

▶ A MTH YST

▶ F CHS

▶ TH ST L

► TRY IT ◄

DAY 35: EXERCISE 3

Can you rearrange the letters in each of the following anagrams to reveal a set of different types of transport? Ignore any spaces – all the vehicles are single words.

► ZL BOULDER

► I TAX

► BY CECIL

► TO SCORE

► KANT

► A MEAN CLUB

► POLE ARENA

► ROT CART

DAY 36

CREATIVE WRITING

+ Overcome writer's block by starting within limits
+ You don't need to begin at the beginning
+ Practise, and don't expect immediate perfection

WHAT?

Have you ever fancied writing creatively, but found it hard to get going when sitting down with pen and paper – or keyboard and screen. Having the ability to write about 'anything' means that so many decisions need to be taken that they can be quite overwhelming.

WHY?

It's much easier to make a decision when you have less to think about, and similarly it's easier to get going when you have fewer decisions to make. Jumping into something without preparation might not seem sensible, but just the very act of starting helps the decision-making process become easier by reducing it to smaller, simpler steps.

Suggested time to spend
18 MINUTES

▶ IN DEPTH ◀

SCALE UP

Start small, then scale up later if you want. Don't agonize over decisions and don't be afraid of keeping things simple. Then, as you begin to write, you will find your story and characters evolving. You can always go back and rewrite your early text so it fits with what your story and your characters later became.

If you have trouble coming up with initial ideas then try limiting your scope. Write about things you know, set in a world you know. Pick character names at random from a list of baby names, or use other techniques to limit the number of decisions you need. You can revisit them later, as your work evolves.

JUMP RIGHT IN

If you have trouble getting going, try starting in the middle of your story – or even at the conclusion – then jumping around and writing the bits you see most clearly. The rest will start to fill itself in as your imagination gets to work on the solid rungs you have created in your story.

WRITE FOR YOURSELF

As with any art, beauty is in the eye of the beholder so it's a good idea to write for yourself rather than others. And if you are writing for yourself, you need not be too concerned about the opinions of others. It also isn't necessarily about *what* you write, but the act of writing itself.

You can also take advantage of the techniques described earlier in this book, such as how exercise can help you come up with creative ideas, or how your brain carries on thinking while you sleep and then can present new ideas the next day.

▶ TRY IT ◀

DAY 36: EXERCISE 1

Try these creative writing exercises, to which there are no right and wrong (or suggested) answers. They're intended purely to give creative writing prompts which are much more restricted, and therefore hopefully easier to get going on, than more general writing tasks.

Start with these half-written poems. Only one line is given, so can you supply a suggested second line? It can rhyme if you like, but it doesn't have to.

▶ Every morn I rise and see,

_____

▶ All the world will know it's true,

_____

▶ Whenever I am lost in thought,

_____

▶ The final thought she had that day,

_____

► TRY IT ◄

DAY 36: EXERCISE 2

Write a (very!) short story involving each of the following plot constraints:

► A dog named Mr Woof

► An Olympic runner named Danny

► A bag left lying on a bench

► A mysterious sound

To help keep the story brief, see if you can fit it into the following space:

_____

_____

_____

_____

_____

_____

_____

_____

EXPANDING KNOWLEDGE

+ The wider your experience, the broader your thinking
+ Try new activities, and challenge yourself
+ Make an effort to learn something new every day

WHAT?

We don't know what we don't know, so the only way to find out is to explore. This exploration need not be physical, although it's great if it is, but can instead involve a wide range of cultural experiences. These could include museum visits, reading overseas newspapers, attending talks, and watching documentaries.

WHY?

Continued learning helps expand your horizons, allowing richer and deeper thought. It's also beneficial for your brain, which loves to be challenged. The more unfamiliar an experience, the better – for example, travel to unfamiliar places typically involves a huge variety of new experiences for all the senses. But even less radical learning is well worth fitting into your day.

Suggested time to spend
15 MINUTES

▶ TRY IT ◀

DAY 37: EXERCISE 1

How many of the fifty US states can you name? Write them on this list:

1: _____   26: _____

2: _____   27: _____

3: _____   28: _____

4: _____   29: _____

5: _____   30: _____

6: _____   31: _____

7: _____   32: _____

8: _____   33: _____

9: _____   34: _____

10: _____   35: _____

11: _____   36: _____

12: _____   37: _____

13: _____   38: _____

14: _____   39: _____

15: _____   40: _____

16: _____   41: _____

17: _____   42: _____

18: _____   43: _____

19: _____   44: _____

20: _____   45: _____

21: _____   46: _____

22: _____   47: _____

23: _____   48: _____

24: _____   49: _____

25: _____   50: _____

▶ TRY IT ◀

DAY 37: EXERCISE 2

How familiar are you with former British Prime Ministers? Can you list the names of the most recent ones? The years they were in office are given as an aid.

▶ 1970–74: _____

▶ 1974–76: _____

▶ 1976–79: _____

▶ 1979–90: _____

▶ 1990–97: _____

▶ 1997–2007: _____

▶ 2007–10: _____

▶ 2010–16: _____

► TRY IT ◄

DAY 37: EXERCISE 3

How many countries in Africa can you name? At the time of writing there are fifty-four sovereign states.

1: _____   28: _____
2: _____   29: _____
3: _____   30: _____
4: _____   31: _____
5: _____   32: _____
6: _____   33: _____
7: _____   34: _____
8: _____   35: _____
9: _____   36: _____
10: _____   37: _____
11: _____   38: _____
12: _____   39: _____
13: _____   40: _____
14: _____   41: _____
15: _____   42: _____
16: _____   43: _____
17: _____   44: _____
18: _____   45: _____
19: _____   46: _____
20: _____   47: _____
21: _____   48: _____
22: _____   49: _____
23: _____   50: _____
24: _____   51: _____
25: _____   52: _____
26: _____   53: _____
27: _____   54: _____

USING YOUR MEMORY

+ Practising using your memory can bring quick benefits
+ Previous generations used to memorize far more
+ Your memory is more powerful than you realize

WHAT?

Now that so many people carry mobile phones around with them, we always have somewhere to make a note of a name, phone number, birthday, address or appointment. Once upon a time we would have kept these in our heads, at least for a little while, but now we no longer need these skills.

WHY?

It makes sense to write down something you might forget, or misremember, but doing so at the exclusion of deliberately using our memories at all causes us to have weaker memory skills than we otherwise would. It's well worth practising remembering things, even if it's just a short shopping list or a set of walking directions.

Suggested time to spend
15 MINUTES

► TRY IT ◄

DAY 38: EXERCISE 1

Try these memory exercises to strengthen your memory skills.

Start by memorizing this shopping list:

► Bread

► Milk

► Cheese

► Newspaper

► Juice

► Yoghurt

► Butter

► Kitchen towel

Take as long as you like. When you think you are ready, cover over the above list and answer the questions below.

► 1. How many items were on the list?

► 2. What two items beginning with 'B' were on the list?

► 3. What two non-food items were on the list?

► 4. Can you write out all of the items that were on the list?

DAY 38: EXERCISE 2

Look over these pictures on the top half of the page, then cover them over and read the second part of this exercise below.

Which of these images do you recognize from above, and which are new?

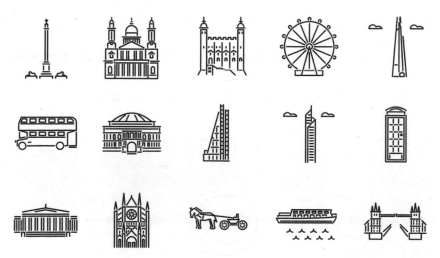

▶ TRY IT ◀

DAY 38: EXERCISE 3

Read through this list of numbers slowly, but without making any conscious effort to memorize them, and then as soon as you reach the last number quickly write them all down in the same order – without looking back.

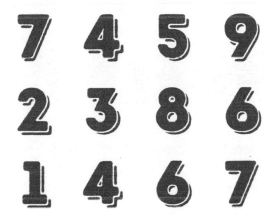

Now check back and see how you did. How many did you remember from the sequence?

DAY 38: EXERCISE 4

Try a similar exercise with these smiley faces. Look at each one in turn, without making any effort to remember it, then turn the book over and try to recreate them on a piece of paper.

SMART REASONING

+ Start with facts, not opinions
+ Consider the reliability of facts
+ Does a conclusion apply in general, or is it specific?

WHAT?

For all but the most trivial decisions, it's often important for decisions to be grounded in facts. Not only does this help ensure they lead to the desired outcomes, but it also provides justification for each decision should it later be needed. However, how do you decide what is and isn't a fact?

WHY?

Some facts are clear. For example, if choosing a new furniture item then you care about the price and the appearance, which you can see for yourself and so be sure of. But how do you judge other factors, such as the quality, sturdiness, durability or environmental implications of the product? If you rely on assurances from a store, are these assurances actually facts or are they simply opinions? What about things you *can't* see?

Suggested time to spend
18 MINUTES

► IN DEPTH ◄

A NUMBERS GAME

It can be very hard to judge the truth of claims that are outside your own ability to assess. Just because you read or hear something a lot of times doesn't make it true – every report could be copied from the same original source, which is nowadays not uncommon in an internet-connected world.

For some facts, however, numbers *are* important. If I count how many red sweets I get in a packet of mixed sweets, this doesn't necessarily tell me anything about other bags. Mine could be unusual. But if I look at *hundreds* of bags, I will get a much better idea of what is normal. The same kind of safety in numbers applies to most observations, and the more complex the thing you are observing then the higher the numbers need to be. Health studies on a few dozen people are rarely of any significance, for example.

GENERAL CONCLUSIONS

Small samples may not allow firm conclusions to be made, but even just a general idea can be helpful in many cases. The danger is in then applying that general idea too specifically, for example by assuming that all sweet bags have a similar distribution of red-coloured items. We may prefer more specific conclusions because they seem easier to comprehend.

Harder to spot is the problem of taking a specific conclusion and misapplying it to different areas where it is not appropriate, or even of reversing a conclusion. This last is often encapsulated by saying that just because carrots are orange, it doesn't mean that everything orange is a carrot. Despite the obviousness of this observation, in real-life situations it is not always clear when this kind of false reasoning is being applied.

DAY 39: EXERCISE 1

Try out your reasoning skills with these puzzles.

Draw along the grid lines to divide the puzzle into a set of rectangles and squares, so that each shape contains exactly one number. That number must be equal to the number of grid squares that make up the shape.

▶ 1.

▶ 2.

► TRY IT ◄

DAY 39: EXERCISE 2

Shade some squares so that a single tetromino (a shape made up of four squares) is formed within each bold-lined area. Tetrominoes must be L, I, T or S shapes, but not a solid 2×2 box. These are the four options:

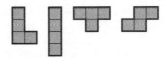

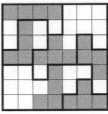

▶ All shaded squares in the puzzle must be connected to form a single area, as in the example solution to the right. Shapes count as connected if they touch, but not counting diagonally.

▶ There may not be any 2×2 areas of squares consisting entirely of shaded squares.

▶ No two of the same type of tetromino (L, I, T or S) may touch (except diagonally). Reflections and rotations of the same type of tetromino still count as the same tetromino, and therefore may not touch.

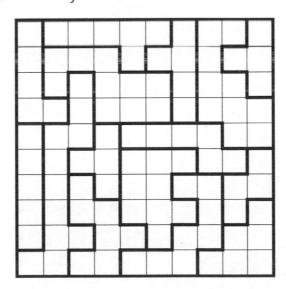

LIFE-LONG LEARNING

+ Take notes on things you wish to remember
+ Continue to challenge yourself as often as possible
+ Seek out new activities and ways to train your brain

WHAT?

Forty days of coaching has only scratched the surface of looking after your brain. It's important to continue the programme you have started with this book by looking for new challenges. Even if those challenges are just to carry on trying out new puzzle types, or improving at those you have already experienced, then you still stand to gain.

WHY?

Your brain needs to be challenged in order to keep functioning at top capacity. Parts that aren't used may be removed in order to streamline its function, so you owe it to yourself to make good use of your brain – every day. You could also seek out the other titles in this *Coach* series, such as the *Memory Coach* book, and try a different 40-day programme.

Suggested time to spend
25 MINUTES

▶ TRY IT ◀

DAY 40: EXERCISE 1

Try this final set of novel puzzle challenges.

Start by filling this sudoku star with numbers, so that each row and column contains the digits 1 to 8 once each, as well as each of the bold-lined 2x4 or 4x2 rectangles.

Each of the rows and columns run in one of three directions, and they bend through 90 degrees when they reach the centre of the star.

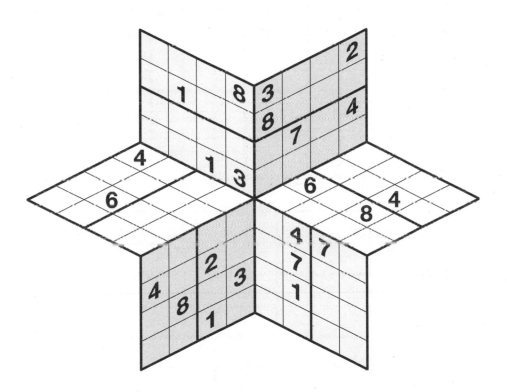

DAY 40: EXERCISE 2

▶ Shade some squares, so that no two shaded squares touch by a side, and all unshaded squares form a single continuous area.

▶ Numbered squares may or may not be shaded, but always give the precise amount of shaded squares in their bold-lined region.

▶ Any continuous horizontal or vertical line of unshaded squares cannot cross more than one bold line.

▶ 1.

2	1				2
	3		0		
			2		

▶ 2.

0			2				
			2			1	
2					3		
		4					
1							

▶ TRY IT ◀

DAY 40: EXERCISE 3

Shade some of the empty squares, and draw a single loop which visits every empty unshaded square. The loop must consist of horizontal and vertical lines, and cannot visit any square more than once. Squares with clues in cannot be shaded and must not be visited by the loop, as per the example to the right.

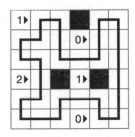

▶ Numbers with arrows indicate the exact number of shaded squares in a given direction in a specific row or column (all the way from the arrow to the end of that row or column, irrespective of other clues), but not all shaded squares are necessarily pointed at by arrows.

▶ Shaded squares cannot touch on a side, although they may touch diagonally.

SOLUTIONS

+ Full solutions are given for all exercises that need them
+ You can use them to check answers or simplify puzzles
+ The puzzles can be beneficial even when not solved

WHAT?

Improving your brain skills requires practice, which is the purpose of the many and varied puzzles in this book. You can get this benefit simply by making a genuine attempt to solve them, however. Actually *reaching* the final solution is not necessarily required.

WHY?

Your brain will gain much of the mental benefit of a puzzle through the process of learning to solve it. Even if your experimentation process doesn't take you all the way to the final solution, you are still learning. It's better to stop before you start to become frustrated, since an unhappy brain does not learn well.

SIMPLIFY?

If a puzzle is proving too challenging, feel free to take a look at the solution for a tip to get you on the way – or an extra clue to copy back into the starting grid, if appropriate.

► SOLUTIONS ◄

DAY 1: EXERCISE 1

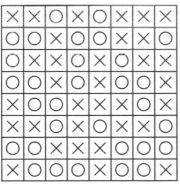

O	O	O	X	O	X	O	X
O	X	X	X	O	X	X	X
O	O	X	O	X	O	O	X
X	O	X	O	X	O	O	O
O	X	O	O	O	X	X	X
X	O	X	O	X	O	O	X
X	X	O	O	X	X	X	O
X	O	O	X	X	O	O	O

DAY 2: EXERCISE 1

- ► NOW/OWN/WON
- ► NAPS/PANS/SNAP/SPAN
- ► EMITS/ITEMS/MITES/SMITE/TIMES

DAY 2: EXERCISE 2

- ► The first net
- ► The fourth net

DAY 3: EXERCISE 1

X	X	O	X	O	X	X	X
O	O	X	O	O	X	X	O
O	X	X	O	X	O	X	X
O	O	X	O	X	O	O	X
X	O	O	X	X	X	O	X
X	X	O	X	O	X	X	O
O	O	X	X	X	O	O	O
X	O	O	O	X	O	O	X

DAY 3: EXERCISE 2

1	1	0	0	1	0	0	1
1	1	0	0	1	0	0	1
0	0	1	1	0	1	1	0
0	0	1	1	0	0	1	1
1	1	0	0	1	1	0	0
0	0	1	1	0	0	1	1
0	0	1	1	0	1	1	0
1	1	0	0	1	1	0	0

1	0	0	1	0	1	1	0
0	1	0	0	1	0	1	1
1	0	1	0	1	0	0	1
0	0	1	1	0	1	1	0
0	1	0	0	1	1	0	1
1	0	1	1	0	0	1	0
0	1	1	0	1	0	0	1
1	1	0	1	0	1	0	0

► SOLUTIONS ◄

DAY 4: EXERCISE 2

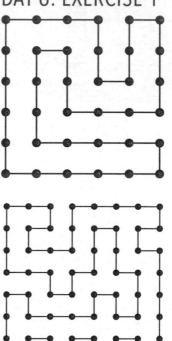

DAY 5: EXERCISE 1

0	1	4	3	0	0	2	2
6	3	2	2	1	2	0	4
5	6	5	2	5	6	0	3
2	4	0	0	3	5	3	6
1	5	3	5	1	3	6	6
4	5	2	4	4	3	6	4
6	5	0	4	1	1	1	1

DAY 6: EXERCISE 1

DAY 5: EXERCISE 2

▶ SOLUTIONS ◀

DAY 7: EXERCISE 1

DAY 7: EXERCISE 2

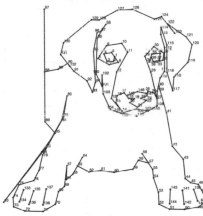

DAY 8: EXERCISE 1

- ▶ A hole
- ▶ A temperature
- ▶ A stamp

▶ You're in second place (not first place)
▶ Darkness
▶ Time
▶ Throw it straight up so it falls back down into your hands
▶ Phone, when you remove the 'p' and 'h', since then it would be 'one'. (Also clone, crone, drone, loner, scone, stone and many others are possible)
▶ On a clock/when adding times
▶ A hole

DAY 8: EXERCISE 2

- ▶ Shift back 1: There is nothing either good or bad but thinking makes it so.
- ▶ Shift back 5: If music be the food of love, play on.
- ▶ Shift forward 3: One touch of nature makes the whole world kin.
- ▶ Shift forward 13: Ignorance is the curse of God; knowledge is the wing wherewith we fly to heaven.
- ▶ Shift back 11: To be, or not to be, that is the question.

► SOLUTIONS ◄

DAY 9: EXERCISE 1

31	32	33	34	35	36
30	29	22	21	20	19
27	28	23	16	17	18
26	25	24	15	14	13
7	8	9	10	11	12
6	5	4	3	2	1

8	7	4	3	58	57	56	55
9	6	5	2	59	62	63	54
10	17	18	1	60	61	64	53
11	16	19	32	33	34	51	52
12	15	20	31	36	35	50	49
13	14	21	30	37	38	47	48
24	23	22	29	40	39	46	45
25	26	27	28	41	42	43	44

DAY 10: EXERCISE 1

F	E	B	D	C	A
E	C	A	F	B	D
D	B	F	E	A	C
A	F	D	C	E	B
B	D	C	A	F	E
C	A	E	B	D	F

A	C	B	D	E	G	H	F
B	G	H	E	F	C	D	A
E	D	A	H	G	F	B	C
D	F	G	A	C	H	E	B
F	H	C	G	B	E	A	D
G	E	D	F	A	B	C	H
H	B	E	C	D	A	F	G
C	A	F	B	H	D	G	E

DAY 10: EXERCISE 2

13	15	17	18	34	35
12	14	16	33	19	36
11	10	9	20	32	31
7	8	1	21	29	30
6	2	23	22	25	28
5	4	3	24	27	26

29	58	57	60	15	16	13	12
30	28	59	56	61	14	17	11
31	27	63	62	55	51	10	18
32	26	64	54	50	52	19	9
33	25	23	49	53	20	8	7
34	24	48	22	21	1	6	5
35	37	40	47	42	45	2	4
36	39	38	41	46	43	44	3

► SOLUTIONS ◄

DAY 10: EXERCISE 3

1	7	6	2	9	8	5	0	4	3
4	9	0	5	3	2	7	1	6	8
0	7	8	1	9	6	4	5	2	3
5	6	3	7	2	0	1	8	9	4
9	8	0	5	1	7	4	2	6	3
19	37	17	20	24	23	21	16	27	21

2	5	1	9	4	8	0	6	7	3
0	9	6	7	3	1	5	2	4	8
8	7	2	1	4	6	0	9	5	3
4	9	5	6	7	2	1	3	8	0
1	8	7	2	4	3	0	5	9	6
15	38	21	25	22	20	6	25	33	20

DAY 11: EXERCISE 4

	2	3	1	2	4	
2	4	3	5	1	2	2
3	1	4	2	5	3	2
1	5	2	1	3	4	2
2	2	5	3	4	1	3
3	3	1	4	2	5	1
	2	2	2	3	1	

DAY 12: EXERCISE 1

DAY 11: EXERCISE 2

- ► The letter 'm'
- ► In a dictionary
- ► The word 'short', when you add 'e' and 'r' to it
- ► It occurs in the middle of every 'day'

DAY 11: EXERCISE 3

16	14	17		23	16	30	
7	8	9	26	8	7	9	
9	6	8	7	6	9	8	17
	8	2	9	5	7	8	
2	1	2	1	8	6	9	
6	8	7	9	2	1	26	17
5	9	7	1	3	2	8	
8	9	7	9	4	6	7	9
7	6	4	9	8	2	4	16
2	1	2	3	8	7		
9	8	6	7	1	5	9	
8	1	2	8	3	16	5	
9	8	6	4	9	7	1	
7	9	8		8	9	4	

DAY 12: EXERCISE 2

► SOLUTIONS ◄

DAY 12: EXERCISE 3

► Words include: erg, ergs, gent, gents, get, gets, gin, gins, girt, girts, gist, grin, grins, grist, grit, grits, ingest, reign, reigns, resign, resting, rig, rigs, ring, rings, sering, sign, signer, signet, sing, singe, singer, sting, stinger, string, tiger, tigers, ting, tinge, tinges, tings and trig.

► Words include: ark, arks, ask, askew, auk, auks, awestruck, cake, cakes, cask, casket, creak, creaks, rack, racket, rackets, racks, rake, rakes, rusk, sack, sake, skate, skater, skew, stack, stake, stark, steak, streak, struck, stuck, suck, sucker, tack, tacks, take, taker, takers, takes, task, teak, teaks, track, tracks, trek, treks, truck, trucks, tuck, tucker, tuckers, tucks, tusk, tweak, tweaks, wake, wakes, weak, wrack, wreak, wreaks, wreck and wrecks.

DAY 13: EXERCISE 2

DAY 13: EXERCISE 3

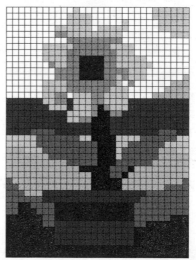

► SOLUTIONS ◄

DAY 15: EXERCISE 2

5	2	4	2	6	2
6	3	6	4	6	1
4	6	2	3	1	5
5	1	5	6	5	3
1	6	6	3	4	2
2	4	3	1	3	6

7	8	3	7	4	1	6	2
4	6	8	2	5	3	7	3
6	2	7	1	3	8	2	5
2	4	6	4	8	4	1	4
1	8	2	6	3	7	2	3
5	4	1	4	2	2	8	6
1	5	2	7	6	1	4	3
8	3	1	5	6	6	2	7

DAY 16: EXERCISE 1

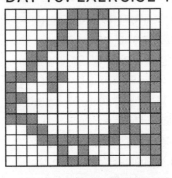

DAY 16: EXERCISE 2

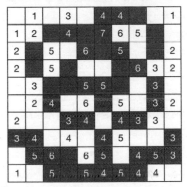

DAY 15: EXERCISE 3

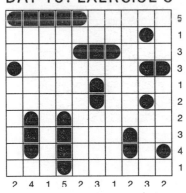

DAY 17: EXERCISE 1

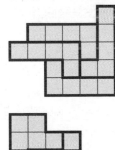

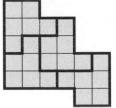

► SOLUTIONS ◄

DAY 17: EXERCISE 2

- ► FARE: WORKFARE and FAREWELL
- ► DOWN: COMEDOWN and DOWNSTREAM
- ► FISHER: KINGFISHER and FISHERMAN
- ► KEY: DONKEY and KEYWORD
- ► PACK: BACKPACK and PACKAGE
- ► WIRE: HAYWIRE and WIRETAP
- ► STATE: REINSTATE and STATEWIDE

DAY 18: EXERCISE 1

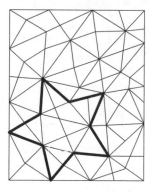

DAY 18: EXERCISE 2

2	4	5 >	3 >	1
1	2	4	5	3
5	1	3	4 >	2
4	3	1	2 <	5
3	5	2	1	4

2	1	6	4	3	5
4	3 >	1 <	2	5	6
5	4	2	3	6	1
6	2	3 <	5	1	4
3 <	6	5	1	4	2
1	5	4 <	6	2 <	3

DAY 18: EXERCISE 3

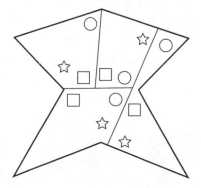

► SOLUTIONS ◄

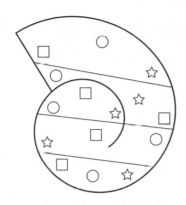

DAY 19: EXERCISE 1

- ► It is January 1st, and my birthday was on December 31st. Currently I am 9, but next year, on December 31st, I will turn 11.
- ► Learning – the other four are all anagrams of one another
- ► Twenty: 5, 15, 25, 35, 45, 50, 51, 52, 53, 54, 55, 56, 57, 58, 59, 65, 75, 85, 95
- ► The ladder was lying flat on the floor at the time
- ► It has all ten digits in alphabetical order
- ► United Arab Emirates (which has eighteen letters)
- ► They are all still words when read backwards: peels; laced; looter; redraw; reviled; snoops
- ► One of the women was a mother *and* a daughter

- ► The mechanism behind a clock

DAY 19: EXERCISE 3

- ► *The Good, The Bad and The Ugly*
- ► *Back to the Future*
- ► *The Lord of the Rings: The Return of the King*
- ► *One Flew Over the Cuckoo's Nest*
- ► *Avengers: Infinity War*
- ► *The Silence of the Lambs*
- ► *Saving Private Ryan*
- ► *Life is Beautiful*

DAY 20: EXERCISE 2

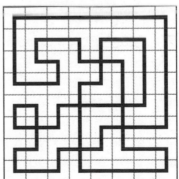

▶ SOLUTIONS ◀

DAY 20: EXERCISE 3

6	5	7	9	3	1	4	8	2
1	8	3	6	2	4	9	5	7
9	4	2	8	5	7	6	3	1
5	9	6	2	7	3	8	1	4
3	1	4	5	8	9	7	2	6
7	2	8	4	1	6	3	9	5
8	3	1	7	6	2	5	4	9
2	7	9	3	4	5	1	6	8
4	6	5	1	9	8	2	7	3

DAY 21: EXERCISE 1

- ▶ ORANGE
- ▶ APPLE
- ▶ RASPBERRY
- ▶ MANGO
- ▶ PEACH
- ▶ APRICOT
- ▶ PLUM
- ▶ BANANA

DAY 21: EXERCISE 2

A & D; B & E; C & F

DAY 22: EXERCISE 1

- ▶ 200 × 150 = 30,000 people could see it
- ▶ 50 / 1000 = 5 / 100 = 5%
- ▶ There are 50 unique followers/friends on each platform, so the maximum number is the 50 shared plus both sets of 50 unique friends/followers, for a total of 150 followers

DAY 22: EXERCISE 2

- ▶ 20 = 4+6+10
- ▶ 26 = 7+8+11
- ▶ 30 = 4+7+8+11
- ▶ 34 = 6+7+10+11

DAY 22:

A letter 'K':

DAY 22: EXERCISE 4

- ▶ Archipelago
- ▶ Peninsula
- ▶ Tundra
- ▶ Savannah
- ▶ Riverbed
- ▶ Glacier

DAY 23: EXERCISE 1

- ▶ 58 = 19 + 13 + 26
- ▶ 70 = 18 + 40 + 12
- ▶ 80 = 30 + 24 + 26

DAY 23: EXERCISE 2

- ▶ 8 ×10 ÷ 5 + 3 = 19
- ▶ 50 − 10 × 4 + 6 + 7 = 173

DAY 24: EXERCISE 1

- ▶ Images found on national flags (e.g. sun on the

► SOLUTIONS ◄

Uruguay flag, trident on the Barbados flag, stars on the US flag, maple leaf on the Canadian flag)
- ► Phonetic alphabet letters
- ► Font terms
- ► Mr Men characters
- ► Gymnastics events
- ► Investment terms
- ► Seas
- ► US state capitals
- ► US presidents

DAY 24: EXERCISE 2

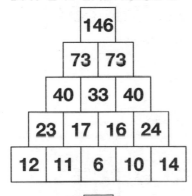

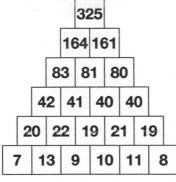

DAY 25: EXERCISE 1

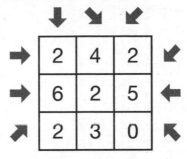

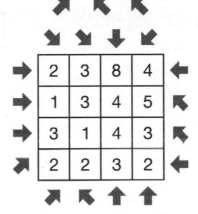

DAY 25: EXERCISE 2

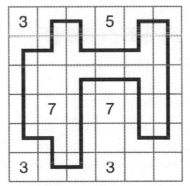

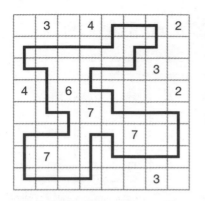

DAY 26: EXERCISE 1

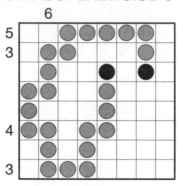

DAY 26: EXERCISE 3

DAY 26: EXERCISE 2

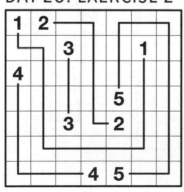

DAY 26: EXERCISE 4

DAY 27: EXERCISE 1

DAY 27: EXERCISE 2

They are both perfectly straight, as you can verify with a ruler or other straight-edged object.

DAY 27: EXERCISE 3

There are no white circles. Your brain infers them from the truncated grid lines.

DAY 27: EXERCISE 4

All three circles are the same size.

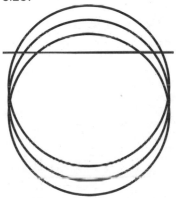

DAY 28: EXERCISE 1

▶ 1992: Barcelona
▶ 1996: Atlanta
▶ 2000: Sydney
▶ 2004: Athens
▶ 2008: Beijing
▶ 2012: London
▶ 2016: Rio de Janeiro

DAY 28: EXERCISE 2

▶ 1967–74: Richard Nixon
▶ 1974–77: Gerald Ford
▶ 1977–81: Jimmy Carter
▶ 1981–89: Ronald Reagan
▶ 1989–93: George H W Bush
▶ 1993–2001: Bill Clinton
▶ 2001–09: George W Bush
▶ 2009–17: Barack Obama

DAY 29: EXERCISE 2

▶ Badminton
▶ Hiking
▶ Dressage
▶ Karate
▶ Snooker
▶ Rodeo
▶ Rugby

DAY 30: EXERCISE 2

1	5	8	7	4	6	2		3
4	9	2	3		5	8	6	7
7	3		2	8	9	4	1	5
2	4	3		5	1	9	7	6
9	1	5	4	6	7	3	2	
6		7	8	3	2	5	4	1
5	8	1	6	7	3		9	2
	7	9	5	2	4	1	3	8
3	2	6	1	9		7	5	4

DAY 31: EXERCISE 1

There are 36 rectangles

DAY 31: EXERCISE 2

1	6	8	5	7	2	4	3
7	5	2	6	1	8	3	4
6	4	3	7	8	1	5	2
4	2	6	8	3	5	1	7
5	7	1	4	2	3	6	8
8	3	4	2	5	6	7	1
2	1	7	3	6	4	8	5
3	8	5	1	4	7	2	6

DAY 31: EXERCISE 3

- 46 cubes
- 33 cubes

DAY 32: EXERCISE 1

- There are most squares
- There are least triangles

DAY 32: EXERCISE 2

The total is 79

DAY 32: EXERCISE 3

The product of 1 to 8 (or 8 to 1) is 40,320

DAY 32: EXERCISE 4

The total is 370

DAY 33: EXERCISE 1

35 = 13 + 22

DAY 33: EXERCISE 2

- 15 = 9 + 6
- 29 = 11 + 13
- 38 = 17 + 21
- 92 = 42 + 50

DAY 33: EXERCISE 3

29	38	57	19	82	62
14	7	25	5	10	3
29	87	58	76	38	19
27	9	3	21	10	5
45	10	7	43	39	95

DAY 33: EXERCISE 4

12× 3	4	16+ 1	5	6	3+ 2
11+ 6	5	12× 3	5+ 2	4	1
3+ 1	2	4	3	11+ 5	6
24× 4	6	1- 5	5+ 1	5+ 2	3
3- 2	36× 1	6	4	8+ 3	5
5	3	2	6	5+ 1	4

9+ 5	1	6× 2	3	8× 4	30× 6
1÷ 6	3	4- 1	96× 4	2	5
3	2	5	6	1	4
432× 4	6	3	4- 1	8+ 5	2
2÷ 2	20× 4	6	5	54× 3	1
1	5	2- 4	2	6	3

▶ SOLUTIONS ◀

DAY 34: EXERCISE 1

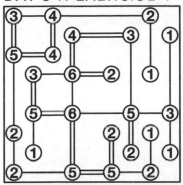

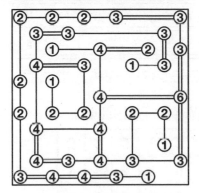

DAY 35: EXERCISE 1

- ▶ Words include aid, aide, ate, die, diet, eat, eta, idea, immediate, maid, mat, mate, meat, media, mediate, mite and tam
- ▶ Words include abase, abased, abases, bad, bade, base, based, bases, bat, dab, data, database, databases, sad, sat and tab

DAY 35: EXERCISE 2

- ▶ MAGENTA
- ▶ LAVENDER
- ▶ INDIGO
- ▶ PLUM
- ▶ AMETHYST
- ▶ FUCHSIA
- ▶ THISTLE

DAY 34: EXERCISE 2

7	6	4	3	2	8	5	1	9
3	8	1	5	6	9	4	2	7
5	2	9	1	7	4	6	3	8
6	4	7	9	8	2	3	5	1
2	5	8	6	1	3	9	7	4
1	9	3	7	4	5	2	8	6
9	1	6	2	5	7	8	4	3
4	7	2	8	3	6	1	9	5
8	3	5	4	9	1	7	6	2

DAY 35: EXERCISE 3

- ▶ BULLDOZER
- ▶ TAXI
- ▶ BICYCLE
- ▶ SCOOTER
- ▶ TANK
- ▶ AMBULANCE
- ▶ AEROPLANE
- ▶ TRACTOR

► SOLUTIONS ◄

DAY 39: EXERCISE 1

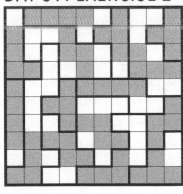

DAY 40: EXERCISE 1

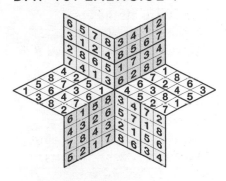

DAY 40: EXERCISE 2

DAY 39: EXERCISE 2

DAY 40: EXERCISE 3

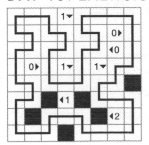

▶ SOLUTIONS ◀

DAY 37: EXERCISE 1

The 50 US states are Alabama, Alaska, Arizona, Arkansas, California, Colorado, Connecticut, Delaware, Florida, Georgia, Hawaii, Idaho, Illinois Indiana, Iowa, Kansas, Kentucky, Louisiana, Maine, Maryland, Massachusetts, Michigan, Minnesota, Mississippi, Missouri, Montana Nebraska, Nevada, New Hampshire, New Jersey, New Mexico, New York, North Carolina, North Dakota, Ohio, Oklahoma, Oregon, Pennsylvania Rhode Island, South Carolina, South Dakota, Tennessee, Texas, Utah, Vermont, Virginia, Washington, West Virginia, Wisconsin and Wyoming

DAY 37: EXERCISE 2

- ▶ 1970–74: Edward Heath
- ▶ 1974–76: Harold Wilson
- ▶ 1976–79: James Callaghan
- ▶ 1979–90: Margaret Thatcher
- ▶ 1990–97: John Major
- ▶ 1997–2007: Tony Blair
- ▶ 2007–10: Gordon Brown
- ▶ 2010–16: David Cameron

DAY 37: EXERCISE 3

The 54 sovereign states in Africa are Algeria, Angola, Benin, Botswana, Burkina Faso, Burundi, Cameroon, Cape Verde, Central African Republic, Chad, Comoros, Democratic Republic of the Congo, Republic of the Congo, Djibouti, Egypt, Equatorial Guinea, Eritrea, Ethiopia, Gabon, Gambia, Ghana, Guinea, Guinea-Bissau, Ivory Coast, Kenya, Lesotho, Liberia, Libya, Madagascar, Malawi, Mali, Mauritania, Mauritius, Morocco, Mozambique, Namibia, Niger, Nigeria, Rwanda, São Tomé and Príncipe, Senegal, Seychelles, Sierra Leone, Somalia, South Africa, South Sudan, Sudan, Swaziland, Tanzania, Togo, Tunisia, Uganda, Zambia and Zimbabwe